The
Salvation
of
The Soul

The
Salvation
Of the Soul

WATCHMAN NEE

Translated from the Chinese

Christian Fellowship Publishers, Inc.
New York

Available from the Publishers at:

11515 Allecingie Parkway
Richmond, Virginia 23235

PRINTED IN U.S.A.

TRANSLATOR'S PREFACE

The subject before the readers of these pages is one which is commonly overlooked by God's people. Yet we are definitely told by the Lord this word: "A salvation ready to be revealed in the last time. . . . Receiving the end of your faith, even the salvation of your souls" (1 Peter 1.5,9). As the end draws nearer and nearer, it is incumbent upon Christians to know what the salvation of the soul is.

In Part I of this latest volume of the author's to appear, Watchman Nee presents to us the meaning, the means, and the manifestation of the soul's salvation: the meaning is self-denial, the means is the cross, and the manifestation is the kingdom. And in Part II he approaches the same subject still further but from a different perspective by showing the sphere of the believer's salvation, the secret of a victorious life, and the faith by which such life is lived.

This book is offered as a companion volume to another work of Mr. Nee's, *The Latent Power of the Soul,** and serves as an answer to the problem discussed in that work of the inordinate power hidden deep within man's soul. Because this latest volume reveals to us God's *positive way* with our soul, it is hoped that the reader may gain from its pages a greater appreciation for the dimensions of God's salvation so graciously given to man.

*Watchman Nee, *The Latent Power of the Soul* (New York, Christian Fellowship Publishers, 1972), translated from the Chinese.

CONTENTS

This volume presents a collection of various messages given by the author in Chinese in the early years of his ministry. The three messages which make up Part One, The Salvation of the Soul, first appeared serially in Chinese during 1930 in the weekly publication of *The Messages* and was reprinted in booklet form in 1974 by The Christian Publishers, Hong Kong. The original sources for Part Two, The Life That Wins, are three booklets that were published in Chinese by the Gospel Book Room, Shanghai, and which bear the same three titles herein adopted.

Scripture quotations are from the American Standard Version of the Bible (1901), unless otherwise indicated.

PART ONE

THE SALVATION OF THE SOUL

1 | Its Meaning: Self-Denial

And the God of peace himself sanctify you wholly; and may your spirit and soul and body be preserved entire, without blame at the coming of our Lord Jesus Christ. (1 Thess. 5.23)

The subject before us is, so far as I know, one which has never been noticed by many people. It is the matter of the salvation of the soul. Whenever we approach the question of salvation there is one thing that is of utmost importance for us to recognize, which is, the tremendous difference between the spirit and the soul. According to 1 Thessalonians 5.23 the Scriptures clearly portray man as possessing three important elements: "your spirit and soul and body". Briefly speaking, the spirit is that faculty by which man is able to commune with God and which none of the lower animals possess. For this reason, the lower animals cannot worship God. The soul, on the other hand, is the organ in man for thought, will, and emotion—something of which the lower animals also share: for the soul speaks of one animal (or animated) life. And lastly, the body is that part of man which communicates with the material world. Since we human beings are composed of spirit, soul and body, our salvation must accordingly reach all these parts.

"That the spirit may be saved in the day of the Lord Jesus" (1 Cor. 5.5). This speaks of the salvation of the spirit. "To wit, the redemption of our body" (Rom. 8.23). This tells of the salvation of the body. But what we would presently like to examine pertains to the salvation of the soul. And to this end, let us carefully examine every place in the New Testament where the salvation of the soul is mentioned so as to enable us to understand what it really means.

> Then said Jesus unto his disciples, If any man would come after me, let him deny himself, and take up his cross, and follow me. For whosoever would save his life shall lose it: and whosoever shall lose his life for my sake shall find it. For what shall a man be profited, if he shall gain the whole world, and forfeit his life? or what shall a man give in exchange for his life? For the Son of man shall come in the glory of his Father with his angels; and then shall he render unto every man according to his deeds. Verily I say unto you, there are some of them that stand here, who shall in no wise taste of death, till they see the Son of man coming in his kingdom. (Matt. 16.24-28)

"Then said Jesus unto his disciples"—By this we know that the following words which the Lord Jesus utters are spoken to His disciples and not to outsiders. If disciples, then they are saved ones. Let us therefore keep in mind that the words which follow are directed at saved saints, not unsaved sinners.

"If any man would come after me"—That is, if any man among the saved would follow the Lord. The man is a saved disciple who wishes especially to follow the Lord. "Follow me" gives the clue to the conditions which are thereafter set forth.

"Let him deny himself"—Denying the self means disregarding one's self or renouncing one's privileges. To deny oneself denotes a setting aside of the self in seeking the mind of God, so that in all things he may not follow his own mind nor be self-centered. Only such kind of people can follow the Lord. This is of course self-evident, for how can anyone follow the Lord if he follows after himself?

"And take up his cross, and follow me"—This is even deeper than denying the self. For self-denying is only the disregarding of self whereas taking up the cross is obeying God. To take up the cross means to accept whatever God has decided for the person and to be willing to suffer according to the will of God. By denying self and taking up the cross we may truly follow the Lord.

"For whosoever would save his life shall lose it: and whosoever shall lose his life for my sake shall find it"—The word "life" here is *psuche* in the Greek original, which means "soul"; and hence this scripture verse tells us about the saving or the losing of our soul. It will give us light on the subject under examination.

"For" connects the following word with what has preceded it. Such connective will help us to see that the phrase "deny himself and take up his cross" in the earlier verse is one and the same thing as saving or losing the soul mentioned in the verse which follows.

"For whosoever would save his *soul*"—Such a rendering therefore means that although he has the desire to follow the Lord he nevertheless is not willing to deny himself and take up his cross. This helps us to understand somewhat the meaning of saving one's soul. It reveals how a person is reluctant to disregard himself, to renounce his privileges and to allow himself to suffer for the sake of obeying God. And thus we can recognize that the meaning of the saving of the soul is just the opposite to the denying of self and the taking up of the cross. If anyone knows what self-denying is and what cross-bearing is, he will also know what saving one's own soul signifies.

The Lord tells us that if any man would be so mindful of himself as to be unwilling to deny his self, take up his cross, and suffer for the sake of obeying God, that one will eventually lose his soul. In trying to save his soul in the above manner, he will as a result lose it in the future. To lose his soul means he will at the end suffer and lose whatever he delights in. He will not obtain what he looks for.

"Whosoever shall lose his life for my sake"—This is the self-denial and cross-bearing spoken of in the preceding verse. Losing the soul is the same as denying the self. The Lord concedes that if for His sake anyone is willing to forsake all the pleasures of the soul and to suffer according to the will of God, he will find the soul. It simply means that whoever is willing for the sake of the Lord to deny his own thoughts and desires so as not to be satisfied with the things of the world but instead to undergo much suffering, he will at another time be given by the Lord his heart desire with full blessing and joy.

By studying this verse we ought to be able to understand what is the meaning of the salvation of the soul. To save the soul denotes gaining for oneself happiness and joy to his heart's fullest satisfaction. To lose the soul, on the other hand, speaks of losing one's joy, desire and satisfaction.

Hence to lose the soul (which requires self-denial and cross-bearing) is definitely not what we commonly term "to perish"; instead, the Lord shows us that to save one's soul is in not denying self and taking up the cross. This concept has no relationship to the ordinary idea of "save" or "perish"—a fact which is quite evident, because if saving one's soul means having eternal life, why does the Lord Jesus declare that a person must lose his soul for the Lord's sake? If losing one's soul suggests a going to the lake of fire, then in requiring us to lose our souls for His sake would He want us to go down to the lake of fire for Him? Consequently, this passage has absolutely nothing to do with the issue of eternal life or the lake of fire. The phrase "shall lose it [the soul]" in the first half of the verse and "shall lose his life [soul]" in the second half of the verse must mean the same. If "whosoever would save his life shall lose it" means that whoever does not deny self will go to the lake of fire, then the words "whosoever shall lose his life for my sake shall find it" would mean that whoever goes to the lake of fire for the Lord's sake shall have eternal life. But this would be absurd. Therefore, what is meant here is simply this: that if a saved Christian will not permit his soul to suffer now his soul will suffer in the future, but that if he is willing to let his soul suffer for the Lord's sake now his soul shall not suffer in the future.

Moreover, if the salvation of the soul *did* mean having eternal life (which it does not), then the losing of the soul would have to denote a going into the lake of fire. But then what the Lord Jesus says would not be consistent with what is said before. For the Lord is here speaking to the disciples, who have already been given eternal life; and we know that a non-Christian can neither deny himself nor take up his cross and follow the Lord. If the Lord desires a person to have eternal life He would no doubt ask that one to believe rather than demand him to deny himself in order to possess eternal life. Only one who has had eternal life is able to deny himself, take up the cross, and follow the Lord. For a sinner who has not yet possessed eternal life, what he needs to do is not to try to follow the Lord but to believe in the Lord.

"For what shall a man be profited, if he shall gain the whole world, and forfeit his life? or what shall a man give in exchange for his life?"—Again, the word "life" is "soul" in the original. Here our Lord continues to explain how unprofitable it is for a man to save his soul now and lose his soul later. What He means is that if one does not deny himself, take up the cross and closely follow the Lord but instead does things according to the desires of his soul in order to satisfy it, there will come a time when he shall lose his soul even though he may have gained the entire world. Though man may gain many pleasures by following his own desires, eventually, says the Lord, he will have to pay back through losing all pleasures to his soul. According to the Lord's viewpoint, it would be far better to gain one's soul at the last than to gain it at the first. Nothing can be exchanged for the final satisfaction of the soul. So that to lose the soul now is far better than to lose it at the end.

"Whosoever would save his life shall lose it"—If a man saves his soul now, when will he lose it? "And whosoever shall lose his life for my sake shall find it"—Again, when will a man find his soul? We see from this same passage that the Lord answers these questions with these words: "For the Son of man shall come in the glory of his Father with his angels; and *then* shall he render unto every man according to his deeds" (v.27).

"According to his deeds" means according to what each does in this present life. Such deeds are divided into two categories: (1) saving his own soul now, and (2) losing his soul now for the Lord's sake. "He shall render unto every man according to his deeds" means that the Lord shall cause the one who saves his soul now to lose it and cause the other who loses his soul now for the Lord's sake to gain it. And when will this happen? At the time of His coming. Therefore, let us be perfectly clear that if a person should mind the things of the flesh, cater to his own pleasure, and refuse to suffer for Christ, he will receive the Lord's reproof instead of receiving the

Lord's glory and may even weep and gnash his teeth at the coming of the Lord. But if he should be willing to forfeit his own rights, be wholly separated from the world, and be faithfully obedient to the will of God, he shall be praised by the Lord and shall enjoy the joy of the Lord to his heart's full satisfaction.

The coming of the Lord and His recompense relate especially to reigning with Him in the kingdom. For the Lord himself informs us immediately with respect to where He is coming. In this same passage He states that "the Son of man [is] coming in his kingdom" (v.28). What the Lord Jesus means to say is that when He shall come to earth to reign for a thousand years, some of the believers will reign with Him while some of them will not.

Hence the gist of this Scripture is to divide into two classes the disciples who have believed in the Lord and possess eternal life. One class denies self and takes up the cross; the other class does not deny self nor take up the cross. One class is willing to forsake all for the Lord and to lose the soul, while the other class seeks to gain the pleasures of the world for self and is unwilling to lose the soul. A disciple of Christ is one whom the Lord has separated out from the sinners. And once again He will separate: this time, separating a self-denying disciple from the non-self-denying one. We ought to know that our future position in the kingdom is decided by our deeds today. Whatever is meant in today's gain will be the meaning of the future's gain; whatever is meant by today's loss will be the meaning of tomorrow's loss. If today's gain means gaining the world and avoiding sufferings, then the future gain for the self-denying one will mean gaining the world without sufferings. If today's loss means forsaking the world and not following one's own will, then future loss for the non-self-denying one will mean losing the world and not getting what one desires. This is what the Lord means: that all who are gratified by the world today shall lose the position of reigning with Him in the future. Consequently, the salvation of the soul is quite different from what we commonly know as the salvation of the spirit (which means having eternal life).

How is the spirit saved? "That which is born of the Spirit is spirit" (John 3.6). We are told in the context of John 3 that he who believes has eternal life. To the believing one, his spirit is saved. Accordingly, the salvation of the spirit means having eternal life. But how is the soul saved? The passage which we have been considering tells us that if we lose our soul for the Lord's sake, our soul shall be saved. And hence the salvation of the spirit is to have eternal life while the salvation of the soul is to possess the kingdom.

The spirit is saved through Christ bearing the cross for me; the soul is saved by my bearing a cross myself.

The spirit is saved because Christ lays down His life for me; the soul is saved because I deny myself and follow the Lord.

The spirit is saved on the basis of faith: once having believed, the matter is forever settled, never again to be shaken. The soul is saved on the basis of following: it is a life-long matter, a course to be finished.

By faith the spirit is saved, because "he that believeth on the Son hath eternal life" (John 3.36). Through works the soul is saved, because "then shall [the Lord] render unto every man according to his deeds" (Matt. 16.27). Once the spirit is saved, eternal life is assured. Though all the demons in hell may rise up to tempt me, they cannot cause me to perish. Though the angels in heaven come down to smite me, neither can they cause me to perish. Nay, even the triune God cannot cause me to perish. Yet as to the salvation of the soul nothing can be assured today, for whether or not the soul will be gained shall be decided at the coming again of the Lord.

The salvation of the spirit is decided today, because by believing in the Lord one has eternal life. The salvation of the soul, however, is to be decided at the coming of the Son of man.

The salvation of the spirit is a current *gift*, for "God so loved the world, that he gave his only begotten Son" (John 3.16). The salvation of the soul, though, is a future *reward* given at the time of the Lord's return to those who have faithfully followed Him.

In order for the soul to be saved a person must have the spirit saved first. Without the salvation of the spirit, there is no possibility of having the soul saved.

Mark 8.31–38

The record in Mark 8.31–38 generally agrees with

what is in Matthew 16.24–28. We will merely point out the slight differences between them.

"Whosoever shall lose his life for my sake and *the gospel's* shall save it" (8.35). Here is added the words "and the gospel's [sake]"—People usually assume that this refers to those who preach the gospel for the Lord. If this were true, would not the preachers be the only ones who would have their souls saved? But what is stated here is simply the gospel and not the preaching of the gospel. What is "the gospel"? None other than "the gospel of Jesus Christ, the Son of God" (Mark 1.1), the "so great a salvation" spoken of in Hebrews 2.3–4, which is the "bringing many sons unto glory" (Heb. 2.10). This is not merely the gospel of liberating those who have been slaves to sin by a spiritual coming out of Egypt but is the glorious gospel of a spiritual entering into Canaan. "Shall lose his life for my sake" (Matthew) is a being constrained by love. "Shall lose his life for . . . the gospel's [sake]" (Mark) is a being moved by one's own future good, which is for the sake of the kingdom.

"For whosoever shall be ashamed of me and of my words in this adulterous and sinful generation" (8.38). This refers to one who is unwilling to lose his soul life, that is to say, one who in this generation will not suffer for the Lord and for His words. In this adulterous and sinful generation it requires the losing of the soul in order to witness to the Lord's words. Unless a person is really willing to lose his soul he will not be able to witness shamelessly for the Lord in this generation. Many of God's children are never willing nor dare to witness before men on behalf of the Lord who has bought them because they are afraid of being ridiculed and want to preserve their faces. This is a keeping of their own soul in this life. Such people are sure to suffer loss in the kingdom. No one who is not willing to lose his life in this age can see the glory of the Lord in the age to come. All who will reign with Christ in the future will have lost their soul today. No one who loses his soul in this present age will fail to gain it in the next age.

Luke 17.26–37

And as it came to pass in the days of Noah, even so shall it be also in the days of the Son of man. They ate, they drank, they married, they were given in marriage, until the day that Noah entered into the ark, and the flood came, and destroyed them all. Likewise even as it came to pass in the days of Lot; they ate, they drank, they bought, they sold, they planted, they builded; but in the day that Lot went out from Sodom it rained fire and brimstone from heaven, and destroyed them all: after the same manner shall it be in the day that the Son of man is revealed. In that day, he that shall be on the housetop, and his goods in the house, let him not go down to take them away: and let him that is in the field likewise not return back. Remember Lot's wife. Whosoever shall seek to gain his life shall lose it: but whosoever shall lose his life shall preserve it. I say unto you, In that night there shall be two men on one bed; the one shall be taken, and the other shall be left. There shall be two women grinding together; the one shall be taken, and the other shall be left. And they answering say unto him, Where, Lord? And he said unto them, Where the body is, thither will the eagles also be gathered together.

In this passage from Luke 17 all the words "life" are "soul" in the Greek original.

Here we are told when the soul shall be saved. "I say unto you, In that night there shall be two men on one bed; the one shall be taken, and the other shall be left. There shall be two women grinding together; the one shall be taken, and the other shall be left" (vv.34–35). This points to the time of *rapture*. The difference here is that one is taken and one is left. To be taken means to be raptured to heaven (cf. Gen. 5.24). Thus the meaning of verse 33 is clear ("Whosoever shall seek to gain his life shall lose it: but whosoever shall lose his life shall preserve it"). He who has saved his soul in this age shall be left behind at the coming of the Son of man, while he who has lost his soul in this age shall be taken at the coming of the Son of man. There does not appear to be any difference between the two persons, neither in work nor in place; yet in rapture there does come a difference! In a twinkling, what a *vast* difference!

A most serious problem is presented here. If we wish to be raptured, to see the Lord, and to enter the kingdom, we must first lose our souls in this age. For the sake of the Lord, we must forsake the world, forsake all which is not in accordance with the will of God, forsake all which will entangle us, and forsake all that would hinder our hearts from thinking on the things above. Should we be like Lot's wife, trying to preserve the soul and unwilling to forsake anything,

we will not be taken up to where the Lord ordains us
to be, even though we may not perish in Sodom and
Gomorrah with the sinners. There may be no difference in eternal life, but there *will* be a difference in
rapture.

Luke 12.15–21

What is meant by losing the soul? We may obtain
an even clearer explanation by reading the following
parable from the Gospel of Luke:

> And he said unto them, Take heed, and keep
> yourselves from all covetousness: for a man's life
> consisteth not in the abundance of the things
> which he possesseth. And he spake a parable unto
> them, saying, The ground of a certain rich man
> brought forth plentifully: and he reasoned within
> himself, saying, What shall I do, because I have
> not where to bestow my fruits? And he said, This
> will I do: I will pull down my barns, and build
> greater; and there will I bestow all my grain and
> my goods. And I will say to my soul, Soul, thou
> hast much goods laid up for many years; take
> thine ease, eat, drink, be merry. But God said
> unto him, Thou foolish one, this night is thy soul
> required of thee: and the things which thou hast
> prepared, whose shall they be? So is he that layeth
> up treasure for himself, and is not rich toward
> God. (12.15–21)

Again, the word "life" here is "soul" in the
original text. We may therefore say that to gain the
soul means to cause the soul to enjoy, to be happy,
and to be satisfied. Contrariwise, though, to lose the

soul means to make the soul suffer—to be pained and poor. This rich man, due to the abundance of his grain and goods, has given his own soul enjoyment, pleasure, and satisfaction in this age. He has already gained his soul now.

Thus to gain the soul is to make it happy in this age, while to lose the soul is to leave nothing to it in this age. What our eyes see, our ears hear, and our hands and feet touch are through our body; but that which is conscious of the pleasures therein is the soul.

The soul is the seat of our natural desires. It enables us to feel and enjoy. The desires of this soul life demand to be satisfied. Beautiful music may soothe the emotion; and literature and philosophy may uplift the thought. Yet if people should seek ultimate satisfaction from these things in this age they will lose satisfaction in the age to come. If we have already received comfort from these things now, we shall lose the glory of the kingdom in the future.

Whoever saves his soul in this age—even if he be a person who believes in the Lord—has already gained the pleasures to be derived from the ears, eyes, and heart; and therefore, in the age to come he shall lose all these pleasures. He who gains now shall lose in the future, while he who loses now shall gain in the future. This is what we should understand about the salvation of the soul. To gain the glory, joy, and satisfaction of the kingdom in the future is to gain the soul. To lose these in the future is to lose the soul.

Having been saved, we obviously may not be "unsaved" ever again. Nevertheless, our deeds have much to do with our position in the future kingdom.

What, then, are we now seeking? How difficult it is for young people to forsake the pleasures of this world. Many seek to find satisfaction in a particular dwelling, in food, clothing, amusements, and so forth. They have already saved their own souls today; consequently, they shall lose their souls in the days to come. One who is already saved will never go down to hell; but he may not enjoy the blessings of the kingdom!

The Lord does not train us to be ascetics; He only would persuade us not to be *captivated* by things of this world. These things may be legitimate, yet not all legitimate things are profitable. Hence Paul says, "All things are lawful; but not all things are expedient [profitable—Darby]" (1 Cor. 10.23). Be it clothing, food, or shelter, we ought not seek for our own enjoyment. We should do all things for the glory of God. If we begin to indulge in these things to excess, we have gone astray.

He who loves the world saves his own soul. Since sin has entered the world, we must not seek anything from this sinful world.

2 | Its Means: the Cross

He that findeth his life shall lose it; and he that loseth his life for my sake shall find it. (Matt. 10.39)

Let us continue with our study of the salvation of the soul. "Think not that I came to send peace on the earth: I came not to send peace, but a sword" (Matt. 10.34). Why does the Lord speak in this way? Because everybody thinks that He comes to send peace to the earth. To correct such a concept, He tells His listeners plainly that He does not come to send peace but a sword. Later on we shall see that the peace mentioned here does not refer to the matter of peace and no war among nations in the world; rather, it alludes to certain situations and relationships in one's family.

"I came not to send peace, but a sword"—What does this word mean? By the sword here the Lord does not have in mind a weapon used in warfare or on the battlefield. He simply states that He comes to give a sword to the earth. Did not Simeon say to Mary shortly after Jesus' birth, "Yea and a sword shall pierce through thine own soul" (Luke 2.35)? And such a meaning in the use of the word sword is what is meant here in Matthew 10. It signifies that all along the way in a person's life he may not sail through smoothly, but on the contrary he will be troubled as though a sword were piercing through his soul. Hence what the Lord is attempting to say is that He comes not to make us enjoy but to have us wounded.

"For I came to set a man at variance against his father, and the daughter against her mother, and the daughter in law against her mother in law" (Matt. 10.35). This verse begins with the conjunctive word "for"—indicating that the words to follow are to explain the "sword on earth" mentioned in the preceding verse. Naturally speaking, the relationship between a father and a son is generally considered to be most congenial, but now such relationship will be marked by alienation. The daughter shall be alienated from the mother, the daughter-in-law shall be alienated from the mother-in-law, and so forth.

"And a man's foes shall be they of his own household" (v.36). Having a foe is to have bitterness. Those of your own household whom you love will turn their faces against you, thus wounding your heart. There will now be hostility and bitterness in your home.

"He that loveth father or mother more than me is *not worthy* of me; and he that loveth son or daughter more than me is *not worthy* of me" (v.37). Twice in this verse are the words "not worthy" spoken by

Jesus. Have you ever wondered why you must love the Lord more than your own father or mother or children? If in the world you love one person more than the Lord, you are not able to be His disciple. To be a disciple of Christ you must love the Lord wholly. This is a condition for being His disciple. It is quite impossible for you to love the Lord and another person equally at the same time.

"And he that doth not take his cross and follow after me, is *not worthy* of me" (v.38). This verse sums up what has been said before—this is a cross! What is meant by taking the cross? The Lord has not said that he who does not take up his burden and follow after Him is not worthy of Him. No, He says that whoever does not take his cross and follow after Him is not worthy of Him. A burden is not a cross. Burden is something inescapable; the cross, however, is subject to personal choice and can therefore be avoided.

What the first cross in history was, so the countless smaller crosses will be which shall follow afterwards: just as the original cross was *chosen* by the Lord, so the crosses for today must also be *chosen* by us.

Some people assume that they are bearing the cross whenever they fall into some hardship or encounter some distress. This is not true, however, for these kinds of things may quite naturally happen to any person even if that person is not a believer. All the crosses one takes up must be *chosen* by oneself. Yet a person needs to guard himself against an error here, which is, that he must not create crosses for himself. We should *take* the cross, not *make* it.

It is therefore a great mistake to consider all which befalls us as constituting crosses for us to take. Whatever crosses we ourselves have created are not to be reckoned as crosses to take.

What then is a cross? It must be akin to what the Lord Jesus himself has said: "My Father, . . . thy will be done" (Matt. 26.42). The Lord asks His Father not to answer as He the Son wills, but as the Father wills. This is the cross. To take the cross is to *choose* the will which the Father has decided. May I say truthfully that if we do not *choose* the cross daily, we have no cross to take up. If the Lord had waited until the cross had come to Him on the earth, how would it have been possible for Him to have been the Lamb slain from before the foundation of the world? For had He not chosen the cross in heaven when He there and then "emptied himself, taking the form of a servant, being made in the likeness of man"? "And being found in fashion as a man, he humbled himself, becoming obedient even unto death, yea, the death of the cross" (Phil. 2.7-8). Our Lord truly *chose* the cross. "No one taketh it [my life] away from me," said Jesus, "but I lay it down of myself. I have power to lay it down, and I have power to take it again" (John 10.18). In accordance with the same principle, our cross must be something which *we ourselves choose*.

In the areas of our clothing, food, and dwelling place we too have our choice. We may choose what to wear, what to eat, and how to dwell. The degree to which we seek these things should only be to the extent of our natural needs in these areas. If we seek to satisfy our lusts with these things, we are not taking up the cross. We may not prescribe who should wear what kind of clothes, eat what sort of food, or live in what type of house; but whoever wishes to derive ultimate satisfaction from these things does not take up the cross. No one dares to tell you what you should have or what you should not have. On the contrary, it is for you to ask yourself if your soul extracts enjoyment and satisfaction from these things.

Anything which supplies your need is permitted by God. Clothing, food, and shelter are all legitimate. In the Old Testament we can see how God provided these things for the children of Israel. Yet He never intended to have His children fully occupied with these matters. If we look for absolute enjoyment in these areas we are not taking the cross.

How often people are clothed not for protecting the body and are eating not for satisfying their hunger but rather for the sake of pure enjoyment. All natural requirements should be supplied; but the lustful demands of the flesh ought not be met. Nothing should be in excess.

Does God really intervene in the clothing, eating, dwelling, and traveling of man? Indeed He does. And such intervention constitutes the cross. Let us illustrate this matter: When Adam was in the Garden of Eden, all his necessary provisions were duly supplied. He could eat the fruits of all the trees except the fruit of one tree which was the tree of the knowledge of good and evil. Now were he to eat of this tree because its forbidden fruit was good for food and a delight to the eyes but not because it would fill his

natural need, this would and did become a "lust" for
him. What God allows is restricted to natural require-
ment; anything in excess of this is improper concerning the things of the world such as clothing, food, and
shelter; and hence we should only seek for the supply
of *needs* and not the gratification of *lusts*! We must
take the will of God as the absolute rule on these
things. Otherwise, we may follow the self-will of the
flesh in either indulging ourselves to the full or else ill-
treating our bodies as though we were holier than
others. We need to see that neither extreme is God-
approved in His word: that He has neither told us that
we are to enjoy wantonly the things of this world nor
declared that ascetic ill-treatment of the body has any
value against the indulgence of the flesh (on the contrary, compare 1 John 2.14–15 and Col. 2.23).

"He that findeth his life [soul] shall lose it; and he
that loseth his life [soul] for my sake shall find it"
(Matt. 10.39). This verse concludes the Matthew 10
passage we have been discussing. What then is meant
by taking the cross? It means for a person to lose his
soul life for the sake of Christ, to be wounded in heart
for Christ's sake and suffer anguish and sorrow—and
all this is a losing of the soul. Some people refuse to
suffer or to discipline their emotional desires; and
thus in allowing their souls to enjoy excessively, they
eventually will lose their souls. Losing the soul for the
sake of the Lord is not letting one's soul be gratified
in its lustful demands and delights. If for the sake of
Christ we give up seeking what we naturally like most,
this will be reckoned as losing the soul for His sake.

Let us recognize that the meaning of the gaining of the soul today applies equally to the gaining of the soul in the future; and the meaning of the losing of the soul now is the same as the losing of the soul then. Their meanings must remain the same. In other words, to lose the soul for the Lord's sake denotes the refusal to allow the soul to be gratified and pleased today, and to lose the soul in the future signifies the denial to the soul of satisfaction and enjoyment in the kingdom. When that day shall come, that is to say, when the kingdom shall arrive, some people will have their souls fulfilled while others will have their souls unfulfilled. All who in this age have catered to their soul's desires by excessive enjoyment beyond the natural needs shall not obtain anything in the future kingdom. Similarly, all who for the Lord's sake lose these things in this age shall be fully satisfied in the kingdom age to come. Everyone who overcomes the world shall be rewarded in the kingdom. This is absolutely certain.

The salvation of the spirit is decided at the time we believe in the Lord. The salvation of the soul depends on what we do today. In case you love clothing, eating, and friends and have all of them to your soul's satisfaction, let me tell you by the authority of the Lord that you will miss the glory of the kingdom. "Blessed are ye that weep now," says the Lord, but "woe unto you, ye that are full now!" (Luke 6.21,25) Why does woe betide those who are full? Because they are already full *now*. Why are those who now weep blessed? Because they shall be filled *in the future.* Such, then, is the difference between woe and blessing.

Luke 14.25-35

"Now there went with him great multitudes: and he turned, and said unto them" (v.25). Why are there such great multitudes going with the Lord? Because He has just preached the gospel. As is indicated in the parable which precedes this verse, He invites a great number of people to come. In fact, all who want to eat have come. Many are the Christians; how very joyous it is to be saved. How good it is to be born again and thus to possess the grace of God. These people go along with the Lord, and to them He turns to speak. The purport of what He will next say is this: Yes, you are saved; but if you want to follow Me, you will now have to fulfill certain conditions. He thus raises the standard of truth, for He will not lower God's ordained yardstick on account of the great multitudes. Can we therefore refrain from speaking of the lofty truths of the kingdom, with its reigning and so forth, because of men?

The door by which to believe in the Lord Jesus and to be saved is wide, but the door by which to follow Him and to be glorified with Him is narrow. "Him that cometh to me I will in no wise cast out" (John 6.37). This is salvation. Yet there are conditions for those who desire to follow the Lord and be His disciples.

"If any man cometh unto me, and hateth not his own father, and mother, and wife, and children, and brethren, and sisters, yea, and his own life [soul] also, he *cannot* be my disciple" (Luke 14.26). Here the Lord rekindles the question concerning the soul. He first mentions father and mother and wife and children and brothers and sisters; then He mentions the soul. If anyone is able to not look at his soul as precious, he is free from all attachments. One ought to lay aside anything that gladdens and pacifies the soul.

The Lord does *not* say that one should cast out his father and mother and wife and children and brothers and sisters. What He *does* say is that one must get rid of his natural life so that he may gather up all his love which he has for other people so as to love the Lord more. This is a must. Before a man begins to follow, a formidable barrier is put up before him by the Lord. If he can surmount this barrier, he will be able to overcome everything in the future. The Lord does not wait to set up that barrier *after* one has entered the door. No, the barrier stands there right from the start. And whoever surmounts this barrier is fit to be the Lord's disciple.

After Christ has saved a person, the first thing which stands at the door of discipleship is this condition. The Lord does not lay down this condition three or five years after a person is born again. Whether a person will be His disciple is a matter to be decided at the very beginning.

"Whosoever doth not bear his own cross, and come after me, cannot be my disciple" (v.27). This explains the preceding verse. What happens is a bearing of the cross.

Then the Lord presents three parables to illustrate the bearing of the cross.

1. The Parable of Building a Tower (vv.28-30)

"For which of you, desiring to build a tower, doth not first sit down and count the cost, whether he have wherewith to complete it?" (v.28) The Lord talks about counting the cost. May we not easily construe this to mean that if we do not have the funds we may as well give up the whole idea of building a tower? Yet if so, the Lord would not have called the great multitudes (who have very little) to follow Him. Is it, then, that because of the lack of funds we do not need to build? Not at all. For if everyone puts in all he has, no one would dare to say there is insufficient funds. What the Lord really means to say here is whether a person is willing to put up *all* he has in order to build a tower. For example, if the building of a tower will cost $500 and a man is only willing to put in $300 while keeping his remaining $200 for other purposes, this cannot be viewed as not having a sufficient fund. It becomes insufficient only because he keeps a part back for purposes other than building the tower. He who keeps back love for others is unable to love Christ. One must hate his own father and mother and wife and children and brothers and sisters—and even his own life—in the sense of taking them out of his heart. Christ does not ask how much a person gives but rather if he has given all to Him.

"Lest haply, when he hath laid a foundation, and is not able to finish, all that behold begin to mock him, saying, This man began to build, and was not able to finish" (vv.29–30). Such will be the end of him who is unwilling to love the Lord wholly. He has to cease building the tower after the foundation is laid because he keeps back something and is not willing to give all to the Lord.

2. The Parable of War (vv.31–32)

"Or what king, as he goeth to encounter another king in war, will not sit down first and take counsel whether he is able with ten thousand to meet him that cometh against him with twenty thousand?" (v.31) To mobilize ten thousand does not mean that ten thousand are all the soldiers the king has. It simply means that he is willing to use *only* ten thousand. Were he to mobilize the entire nation he no doubt would be victorious.

"Or else, while the other is yet a great way off, he sendeth an ambassage, and asketh conditions of peace" (v.32). This is to say that if the king is not willing to throw in all his troops, it is far better for him to ask for conditions of peace and to acknowledge his defeat.

Whoever is willing to put in *all* in building or in war will find everything just right; but if he should keep back a little, he will experience just that much insufficiency. Suppose I go to a book store to buy a Bible, and it costs 60 cents which is just what I have. If I only pay 10 cents, this naturally is not enough; but even if I pay 59 cents and merely keep back one penny this still is not enough. It is therefore absolutely certain that whoever does not take up his cross and follow the Lord wholly is not worthy nor capable of being a disciple of the Lord.

Not due to insufficiency, but because of keeping back a little. Now this not keeping back anything is the cross. We must lay everything on the cross. Some may ask how do we know that this parable teaches the necessity of laying all on the cross? Because this is what the Lord himself explains in the following verse.

"So therefore whosoever he be of you that renounceth not all that he hath, he cannot be my disciple" (v.33). This verse comments on the above two parables. The problem with these two persons already mentioned does not lie in their not having enough but in their not being willing to spend all. How frequently we want both; we are so double-minded as to love the world on the one hand and to love the Lord on the other. For us to love the Lord entirely, this we cannot do; yet to love only the world is something we feel ashamed of as being unfair to the Lord. In anyone's unwillingness to spend all to build the tower and yet being apprehensive of not spending at least a little, the outcome will be to have the foundation laid but with the tower unfinished. In being unprepared to commit all one's fighting men, the only course left to a person is to send an emissary to ask for terms of peace. Such people need not consider the matter of being the Lord's disciples. To be a disciple of Christ, one must renounce all he has. He cannot hold on to the world with one hand and with the other hold on to the Lord. He must lay down one side or the other—and if not the world, then Christ.

3. The Parable of Salt (vv. 34–35)

This parable depicts the consequences of these two classes of people about whom we have just discussed. According to Matthew 5.13 ("Ye are the salt of the earth"), salt here in Luke must point to the Christian.

"Salt therefore is good: but if even the salt have lost its savor, wherewith shall it be seasoned?" (v.34)—Salt is good, for it is profitable to men. "Savor" speaks of being set apart and sanctified. What is of tremendous importance to a Christian is to be separated from the world. If salt has lost its savor, how can it be seasoned again? For example, a man buys a piece of fresh meat and thinks of seasoning it with salt. If there is no salt, what can he do to make the meat salty? Or if the salt itself has lost its salty savor, how can he make salty meat?

"It is fit neither for the land nor for the dunghill: men cast it out" (v.35a). This verse speaks of the consequence of our losing our Christian savor, even losing our separation from the world.

"Land" represents the kingdom. To place a savorless Christian in the kingdom of God is most unfit.

"Dunghill" is a defiled and unclean place, and hence suggests hell or the lake of fire. To put a Christian who has lost his savor into hell is equally unfit, for he is already saved.

"Cast it out"—Since he is unfit for either the kingdom or for hell, he must be cast out; that is to say, he must be cast out from the glory of the kingdom.

"He that hath ears to hear, let him hear" (v.35b).

This is a word of warning. Anything which causes us to be disjointed from Christ causes us to lose our proper savor. Savor is strength, savorlessness is weakness. How very serious is this matter! We must not love the world. We must instead love the Lord—and with our whole heart. Otherwise, we will have no part in the kingdom. The question is not how much have I done, but am I on the altar. Let us consecrate ourselves to the Lord today, for it will be too late when that day (the day of His coming) arrives.

All three parables inform us of the life of a believer who does not lose his soul today. The reason for not spending all the funds to build a tower, for not mobilizing all the forces to fight a battle, and for becoming savorless salt through mingling with the world is the love of one's own soul, is a not being willing to let self suffer or to forsake the loveliness of the world. To such a person as this, the glory of the future kingdom is only dimly seen because he cares only for the present moment. Were he willing to deny the demands of his own soul by denying himself, taking up the cross and doing the will of God, it would not be hard for him to build or fight, to hate his father, mother, wife, children, brothers, sisters, and even his own life, and to be separated wholly from the world to become salt with savor. If in this age we do not lose our soul but instead do what we like, or if our consecration is imperfect, we will be cast out during the kingdom time and be mocked as having failed in discipleship.

3 | Its Manifestation: the Kingdom

In your patience ye shall win your souls. (Luke 21.19)

He that loveth his life loseth it; and he that hateth his life in this world shall keep it unto life eternal. (John 12.25)

But we are not of them that shrink back unto perdition; but of them that have faith unto the saving of the soul. (Heb. 10.39)

Receiving the end of your faith, even the salvation of your souls. (1 Peter 1.9)

In reading Luke 21.5–19 we can readily perceive that this passage of Scripture speaks of the salvation of the soul: "In your patience ye shall win your souls" (v.19). Whenever the Bible talks about our salvation, it usually stresses belief. Here, though, it says that by patience we shall win our souls. There must consequently be a difference between the salvation of the soul and the salvation of the spirit.

If I remember correctly, the Gospel according to John mentions on 35 occasions that he who believes has eternal life. In the entire New Testament there are no less than 150 instances wherein there appear such statements as believe and be justified, believe and have eternal life, believe and be saved, and so forth. Here, however, it speaks of patience. Patience is work, not faith. Hence the salvation of the soul is quite different from simply having eternal life.

Let us read carefully and consider how this passage in Luke 21 speaks of the salvation of the soul.

"And as some spake of the temple, how it was adorned with goodly stones and offerings, he said, As for these things which ye behold, the days will come, in which there shall not be left here one stone upon another, that shall not be thrown down. And they asked him, saying, Teacher, when therefore shall these things be? and what shall be the sign when these things are about to come to pass?" (vv.5–7) The temple mentioned is the holy temple in Jerusalem. "Ye" refers to the disciples. "These things" points to the destruction of the temple in the days—that the Lord Jesus says shall come—when no stone shall be left atop another. Verse 7 deserves special attention. The question there appears to be similar to that which is recorded in the parallel passage of Matthew 24, yet there is a great difference between them. Let us therefore compare these two most closely.

"And as he sat on the mount of Olives, the disciples came unto him privately, saying, Tell us, when shall these things be? and what shall be the sign of thy *coming*, and of the *end of the world*?'' (Matt. 24.3) Matthew speaks not only of the destruction of Jerusalem but also of the coming of the Lord and the end of the world; whereas Luke 21 deals exclusively with the destruction of Jerusalem. In Luke, the disciples ask only when these things shall be (that is to say, when the destruction of Jerusalem is to occur) and what shall be the sign when these things are about to come to pass. There is not a word put forth inquiring about the Lord's coming or the end of the world. Let us remind ourselves that in Matthew questions are raised on these items: (1) When shall these things be? (2) What shall be the sign of the Lord's coming? and (3) What shall be the sign of the end of the world? In Luke, on the other hand, inquiry is made on but one item; that is, When shall these things be and what is the sign when these things are about to come to pass? And hence the question recorded in Luke is the same for only the first question mentioned in Matthew.

The destruction of Jerusalem was subsequently fulfilled in 70 A.D. What the Lord declared with respect to a stone not being left upon another has long since been accomplished.

"And he said, Take heed that ye be not led astray: for many shall come in my name, saying, I am he; and, The time is at hand: go ye not after them. And when ye shall hear of wars and tumults, be not terrified: for these things must needs come to pass first; but the end is not immediately" (Luke 21.8-9). This is what the Lord warns His disciples to be careful about during the period of the soon-to-occur destruction of Jerusalem. Church history proves that after the ascension of the Lord Jesus there were many who falsely claimed themselves to be Christ. And so the Lord wants His own to know that though many will falsely proclaim themselves as Christ and though there will be news of wars and tumults, the end is yet to come.

"Then said he unto them, Nation shall rise against nation, and kingdom against kingdom; and there shall be great earthquakes, and in divers places famines and pestilences; and there shall be terrors and great signs from heaven. But before all these things, they shall lay their hands on you, and shall persecute you, delivering you up to the synagogues and prisons, bringing you before kings and governors for my name's sake" (vv.10–12). All these were fulfilled in the apostolic age: how the disciples were arrested, persecuted, scourged, and imprisoned—and how they were brought before kings and princes.

"It shall turn out unto you for a testimony" (v.13). They so suffered in order that they might have the opportunities to witness. How they indeed testified in the synagogues. How Paul witnessed before Felix and also before those in Rome.

"Settle it therefore in your hearts, not to meditate beforehand how to answer: for I will give you a mouth and wisdom, which all your adversaries shall not be able to withstand or to gainsay. But ye shall be delivered up even by parents, and brethren, and kinsfolk, and friends; and some of you shall they cause to be put to death. And ye shall be hated of all men for my name's sake. And not a hair of your head shall perish" (vv.14-18). Here the Lord prophesies what they will experience later.

"In your *patience* ye shall *win your souls*" (v.19). In this last matter, the disciples are held responsible. When all these sufferings and persecutions come upon them, they need to keep their patience. And thus shall they win their souls.

Now this matter of the winning of our souls means nothing less than reigning with Christ and enjoying glory together at the return of our Lord. For should the winning of our souls mean the same as our having eternal life, then what is said in verse 19 here ("In your patience ye shall win your souls") would be totally incomprehensible. By believing, one shall have eternal life; and thus he is saved. But in verse 19 we are told that in winning one's soul a person must endure with patience all these sufferings.

John 12.25

"He that loveth his life [soul] loseth it; and he that hateth his life [soul] in this world shall keep it unto life eternal"—The Lord tells us that one may lose his soul for the single reason that he loves his own soul.

What is meant by loving our souls? It is to gratify all our desires and to please all our passions. If the Lord, for example, calls us to leave off doing a certain matter, we need to lay down ourselves so as to obey the Lord. Each time we obey Him, each time we must lay down ourselves. In seeking to obey the Lord's will we will not succeed should we love our own souls. As a further example, should the Lord want us to forsake this thing or that person that we fondly love, would we ever follow Him if we love our souls? How frequently we are entangled with either a person or a thing or a matter. Many are beset by friends; they refuse to let their souls go unfulfilled.

We need not mention many obviously wrong things for we are well aware of them being sinful. But the things in which we usually take great delight are things about which we are insensitive as to our being entangled. We know money is a word too ignoble to be mentioned; yet how many people there are who are unwilling to part with it! A dress or a delicious delicacy may ensnare a person. Why is it so hard for man not to love his own soul? Because in not loving his soul, he deliberately causes it to suffer. To love his soul is not to allow it to suffer. Yet in so doing, such a person will invariably lose his soul! For he has already yielded to his soul's excessive desires and caused it to enjoy itself.

When will his soul suffer loss? At the time when the Lord shall set up the kingdom. Whoever loves his soul in this age will not be able to enjoy glory with the Lord in that future time. We believe that the possession of eternal life as well as our entering heaven are matters both certain and positive. But as to the matters of reigning in the millennial kingdom and experiencing future enjoyment in the soul—these require of us that we not love our souls today.

I have stated before and I will now state it again that just as God places heaven and hell before the *sinner* for him to choose (and if a sinner can see clearly, he no doubt will choose heaven), so God also places the kingdom and the world before the *Christian* for him to choose. Do we choose the kingdom? Or do we choose the world? How sad that a sinner likes to choose heaven, whereas numerous Christians would rather have the world! Too many of us think being saved is enough; yet let us realize that after we are born again God places the future kingdom before us for us to choose.

He who is full now shall lose fullness in the glory and shall enjoy no more. "He that loveth his life loseth it," declared the Lord, "and he that hateth his life in this world shall keep it unto life eternal"—How closely knit is our soul to the world! To love the soul in this world is to gratify oneself in this world. Eating and dressing well, having many friends and fans, and enjoying fame and praises among men—all these are desirable, but how they do nourish one's soul! Yet whoever nourishes his soul now shall lose it in the kingdom.

To lose the soul is not a going to hell but a causing the soul to suffer in that it cannot reign with the Lord. During the kingdom age the Lord will assign ten cities or five cities to His disciples to rule. According to Old Testament prophecies, this will be the golden age. How very good and pleasant will the ruling over ten or five cities be at such a time! Yet he who has gained his soul in this world shall lose his soul in this regard during the kingdom age. And how serious must this be! All who are filled in this present age—that is to say, all who have their souls satisfied now—will have nothing in the kingdom. I have said many times and I will continue to say it: He who hates his own soul in this age—by which I mean not allowing his soul to be filled and gratified in this age but instead turning his back on the world and turning his face towards God and always arming himself with the will to suffer—shall gain his soul in the kingdom; but he who gains on this side shall lose on the other side. Whoever possesses today shall possess nothing in the future. In order to gain in the future, one must forfeit something today.

To be saved and have eternal life is definite because every believer shall enter New Jerusalem. But before the old heaven and earth shall have passed away, some believers will have had no part in the kingdom, because only "he that hateth his life [soul] in this world shall keep it unto life eternal." Let us notice that the Lord hates two things: First, He hates our sins; and second, He hates our soul life—which is to say, our self life. Because He hates our sins, He dies for us that in believing into Him we may have eternal life. And because He hates our soul life, He will get rid of this soul life of ours (not, please note, ridding us of our soul nor even its functions), that we may enter the kingdom.

Here lies the difference between the soul and sins: What the soul loves may not be sinful. Lying, pride, jealousy, and such like are no doubt sins; but to dress extravagantly and to eat indulgently are actions which pertain to the soul. To dress luxuriously, to eat exorbitantly and to spend lavishly may not be labeled as sins, but they certainly give opportunity to the soul to enjoy itself wantonly.

Madame Guyon in the 17th century was most profound in the Lord. She knew clearly the difference between sins and the soul. Though she did not explain it in the same way, nevertheless her experiences bore out this difference. She was born and reared in France, and her family moved in the circle of the nobility. Now each time she went to Paris she was full of fear lest her inside would be stirred by what she saw there. Later on, Madame Guyon had complete victory over such temptation. She had another fear, however, which was of looking at a mirror; for she was such a beautiful woman, that the more she would look into the mirror the more she was conscious of her beauty. Even the way she carried herself while walking was far more exquisite than that of other women. Surely now, the experiences of this woman serve to illustrate the life of the soul. The soul is the very nature of man.

By believing in the Lord and thus overcoming sins, man can enter heaven. But in purifying the soul by putting away the soul life, man may enter the kingdom. The reason why God would not have us dress too fashionably, eat too delicately, or dwell too luxuriously in this age is that we might not be contaminated by the world, because all these have been infected by it. How easy for us to fall into this world's mold through the way we may dress or eat or be sheltered. But when the kingdom shall come, we may more fully appreciate the beauties of nature inasmuch as they will only cause us to praise the creative powers of God more. Yes, in that day we may even appreciate ourselves more, for we shall realize that what we have become is the result of God's salvation—and this will thus draw out from us more praises to Him. In the kingdom Satan is bound and imprisoned and righteousness shall reign over the earth.

When the Son of God was on this earth, the cross was the only thing that He had as a possession; all the rest He borrowed. The manger was borrowed, the inn was borrowed, the ass on which He róde to Jerusalem was borrowed, the room in which He ate the Passover feast was borrowed, and finally the tomb in which He was buried was borrowed. Everything in the world except the cross was borrowed by the Lord. Yet how very unlike Him we are!

It is certain that all who overcome sins enter heaven and all who overcome the world enter the kingdom. God is calling us to deny the world and seek the kingdom, to hate our self life and love the kingdom.

Hebrews 10.38–39

"But my righteous one shall live by faith" (v.38a). The righteous one here is he who believes in the Lord Jesus and is saved: people such as you and I. To "live by faith" means that the saved sinners must live day after day by faith.

"And if he shrink back, my soul hath no pleasure in him" (v.38b). The "he" points to the righteous one mentioned earlier. Only a believer has the possibility of shrinking back. This righteous one who is already saved is able to shrink back. The word "my" refers to God, for God is not pleased with a regressive righteous person.

"But we are not of them that shrink back unto perdition; but of them that have faith unto the saving of the soul" (v.39). To what extent will this shrinking back be? We who have believed shall never perish since we have *eternal* life; yet we have the possibility of shrinking back to perdition. What, then, is this perdition? It does not mean a becoming unsaved; rather, it means a losing of everything, a being torn down to the foundation and having all things shaken. "But of them that have faith unto the saving of the soul"—Here again the Bible speaks of the salvation of the soul, and once more a choice is put before us. We may either shrink back to perdition or press on to the saving of the soul.

Some people consider the phrase "shrink back unto perdition" to be very objectionable, and therefore they maintain that such words do not apply to Christians. Yet only *Christians* may shrink back; sinners are so far back already that it can rightly be asked, To where can they shrink back any further? All who do not believe in the Son are already condemned. Christians alone have the possibility of drawing back. What a believer does on earth ought to be rewarded. Nevertheless, if he shrinks back, he shall suffer loss. Even though he may preach in the Lord's name, cast out demons in the Lord's name, and perform many wonders and miracles in the Lord's name, the Lord will not recognize him but rather will say to him, "I never knew you: depart from me, ye that work iniquity" (Matt. 7.23).

"But we are not of them that shrink back unto perdition; but of them that have faith unto the saving of the soul"—The saving of the soul is due to faith. What kind of faith is this? What is meant by having faith to the saving of the soul? Let us read Hebrews 11, which declares: "Now faith is the *assurance* of *things* hoped for, a *conviction* of *things* not seen" (v.1). This is the faith that saves the soul, the faith by which the righteous one lives: for please note that chapter 11 follows immediately after the end of this chapter 10 which we have been discussing. This faith is "the assurance of things hoped for" and not the faith of believing in Jesus. This is the kind of faith which may save our soul. This faith is "a conviction of things not seen" and not a belief in the Lord Jesus Christ. Many times the apostle John is found saying "he that believeth on the *Son* hath eternal life"; he speaks of believing in the Lord. Yet here, the Bible speaks of *things* hoped for and not seen.

What are these things? Let us read further into Hebrews chapter 11: "These all died in faith, not having received the promises, but having seen them and greeted them from afar, and having confessed that they were strangers and pilgrims on the earth. For they that say such things make it manifest that they are seeking after a country of their own. And if indeed they had been mindful of that country from which they went out, they would have had opportunity to return. But now they desire a better country, that is, a heavenly: wherefore God is not ashamed of them, to be called their God; for he hath prepared for them a city" (vv.13-16). Do we now see it? Here we are told what kind of faith this is. It is a believing that God has prepared for them a city in the kingdom, a believing that in this world they are but strangers and pilgrims, a believing that their home country is not in this world, and a believing that their inheritance is in the future and not in this present age. This strong city will never fall down. The righteous believe in this fact day by day, and they day by day live by this faith. And in so doing, the soul is being saved by such faith. What a pity that many believers forget that they are only strangers and pilgrims in this age!

James 1.17–21

"Every good gift and every perfect gift is from above, coming down from the Father of lights, with whom can be no variation, neither shadow that is cast by turning. Of his own will he brought us forth by the word of truth, that we should be a kind of firstfruits of his creatures" (vv.17–18). Verse 17 speaks of gift, while verse 18 speaks of how God begets us by the word of truth so that we should be a kind of firstfruits of His creatures. These two verses fit together. For verse 17 tells us how God gives us gift, and verse 18 shows us that this gift is none other than the eternal life which God gives to us. All this indicates that the people who received this letter of James had already had this gift, having been begotten of God by the word of truth—saved in order to become firstfruits.

"Ye know this, my beloved brethren. But let every man be swift to hear, slow to speak, slow to wrath: for the wrath of man worketh not the righteousness of God. Wherefore putting away all filthiness and overflowing of wickedness, receive with meekness the

implanted word, which is *able to save your souls*"
(vv.19–21). In calling them "beloved brethren"
James intimates that these are all saved individuals.
What he tries to impress on them is this: that you
people have already been born again and you know it,
but this alone is not complete since you must "receive
with meekness the implanted word, which is able to
save your souls"—Here he shows us clearly that a
person may be born again and yet his soul may not be
saved until he receives that word which is able to save
his soul. Hence the saving of the soul is something
added beyond regeneration. (Without regeneration,
of course, there is no possibility of having the soul
saved.) God gives us this implanted word which is the
gospel of the kingdom. It tells us that we need to lose
our souls today. As we have said repeatedly, we can
do nothing; even so, if we are willing to let the Holy
Spirit work, He is well able to do all things.

Actually the principles behind the possessing of
eternal life and the saving of the soul are the same. If
a sinner does not want to be saved, he will not be
placed in heaven by God. Indeed, "he that will, let
him take the water of life freely" (Rev. 22.17); but he
who refuses to come to the Lord has no way to be
saved. Likewise, if we are not willing to lose our
souls, the Lord will not be ready to put us in the
kingdom. Unless we ask the Lord to make us willing
to lose our souls, even He cannot do anything for us.

1 Peter 1.3–9

"Blessed be the God and Father of our Lord Jesus

Christ, who according to his great mercy *begat us again* unto a living hope by the resurrection of Jesus Christ from the dead, unto an inheritance incorruptible, and undefiled, and that fadeth not away, reserved in heaven for you'' (vv.3–4). Because of these two verses we can be assured that the people who received this letter were already regenerated.

"Who by the power of God are guarded *through faith* unto a *salvation ready to be revealed in the last time*" (v.5) What kind of faith is spoken about here? It is the same faith as the living by faith mentioned in Hebrews 10.38. Although they are already saved, they are not yet in possession of the salvation ready to be revealed in the last time. It is good to be regenerated, but this is still not enough unless it is accompanied by the salvation ready to be revealed in the last time.

"Wherein ye greatly rejoice, though now for a little while, if need be, ye have been put to grief in manifold trials, that the proof of your faith, being more precious than gold that perisheth though it is proved by fire, may be found unto praise and glory and honor at the revelation of Jesus Christ: whom not having seen ye love; on whom, though now ye see him not, yet believing, ye rejoice greatly with joy unspeakable and full of glory" (vv.6–8). These verses explain how in view of the salvation to be revealed in the future we may rejoice greatly with joy in the midst of fiery trials.

"Receiving the *end of your faith*, even the *salvation of your souls*" (v.9). This word speaks plainly of the salvation of the soul. Peter also confirms that a regenerated person needs to receive another salvation, which is the salvation of the soul. When shall this salvation be obtained? In *the last time*, which commences with the appearing of the Lord Jesus on earth. To us who are saved, the ultimate destiny is the same, but there will be differences in the kingdom. Truly we are saved by believing in the Lord; nevertheless, in addition our souls need to be saved.

1 Peter 2.11

"Beloved, I beseech you as sojourners and pilgrims to abstain from fleshly lusts, which *war against the soul*"—Fleshly lusts war against the soul in order to block its salvation.

1 Peter 2.25

"For ye were going astray like sheep; but are now returned unto the *Shepherd and Bishop of your souls*"—We must lay hold of this verse, knowing that there is a Shepherd and Bishop of our souls.

Finally, we can suggest two more scripture passages for our consideration:

(1) "For the time is come for judgment to begin at the house of God: and if it begin first at us, what shall be the end of them that obey not the gospel of God? And if the *righteous is scarcely saved*, where shall the ungodly and sinner appear? Wherefore let them also that *suffer according to the will of God commit their souls in well-doing unto a faithful Creator*" (1 Peter 4.17–19). May we truly lay hold of

God's word. We have already become the house of God; and yet judgment shall begin at the house of God. Some of the righteous are scarcely saved! Hence let us who suffer according to the will of God commit our souls to the faithful Creator! We ought to be so determined that we shall leave nothing for our soul nor seek to gratify its desires but to suffer according to God's will.

(2) "Wherefore, brethren, give the more diligence to make your calling and election sure: for if ye do these things, ye shall never stumble: for thus shall be *richly supplied unto you the entrance into the eternal kingdom of our Lord and Savior Jesus Christ*" (2 Peter 1.10-11). These people are being addressed as brethren, thus indicating that they are already born again. Nevertheless, it is further pointed out that they need to be more diligent in order to make their calling and election sure. Having eternal life is having something immovable; but in the kingdom some people may be removed.

Let us compare these two phrases—*scarcely saved* and *richly supplied to you* the entrance into the eternal kingdom of our Lord and Savior Jesus Christ. The one phrase speaks of a person as being barely saved—there is hardly anything more to it than a just being born again. It is not unlike a school examination in which 70 is the passing mark, and a student after taking the examination gets exactly 70 and not a point more. Spiritually speaking, how pitiful is such a performance, for it can almost be viewed as someone being merely half-saved. We instead ought to be those who can enter the kingdom richly supplied.

Just here we can use a story to illustrate this point. Immediately after the Great War in Europe, a great celebration was held in London where the number of spectators surpassed anything before known in the history of that city. The war had just been concluded, and the soldiers had returned home for a triumphant march. They were warmly welcomed by the entire nation; and wherever the soldiers passed, there was great applause and much praise. For in the mind of the people, except for the bravery of these soldiers, England might not have been saved. As the soldiers marched on, the sound waves of applause and praise flowed incessantly. Rank after rank had passed by until suddenly the air was explosive with the tremendous waves of even greater applause and praise. Many who watched were moved to tears. And at one point the nobility saluted and the king removed his crown. And why? Because immediately behind the marching ranks came carrier after carrier of soldiers who had lost their limbs or had been terribly wounded in body! Now when these wounded men passed by, they were the ones who received the highest honor and the greatest praise; because the soldiers who had marched ahead of the maimed and injured had passed on, but the glory they had received was far far less than that received by the wounded.

Many who are scarcely saved will enter heaven in the future yet they shall not be able to enter the kingdom of God richly. But for those who have suffered on earth and have forsaken something for the sake of Christ, they shall receive much on that day just as had the wounded soldiers received much during that triumphal march in London: louder applause, higher praise, and greater glory. May each one of us suffer for Christ, that crowns may be placed on our heads in that day. But for such a thing to happen, our souls must be saved. Let us be poorer, let us be wounded, let us suffer more and forsake everything for the Lord's sake. May God bless us.

PART TWO

THE LIFE THAT WINS

1 | The Sphere of Salvation for a Believer

We all know ourselves as having been sinners who have received eternal life through faith. Today we would like to see to what extent Gods saves us through Jesus Christ. In other words, what position will we as individuals arrive at through the salvation accomplished by Jesus Christ.

In recent years one thing has gripped me, which is, that I have sensed that something is wrong in my personal Christian life. For when I read the Bible, I must acknowledge that I do not have what the Book has said I should have. Although there are indeed Christians whose lives are poorer than mine, and even though I have been assured by some who have had deep experience with the Lord that I have already possessed what I should have, nevertheless I still am aware of not possessing all which the word of God says I should have. Thank God, I now know that there are truly things *still more excellent* in Christ for me and that all these things are *obtainable* and may be obtained *now.*

Hence what I would like to share today concerns the scope of our inheritance in Christ Jesus. However, I will not speak on the matter of our inheritance in heaven which we will have in the future, nor on the subject of eternal life which we already possess in regeneration, nor even on the glory of the kingdom which we shall enjoy in the millennium. No, what I will lay stress on here is the extent of what God can do for you and me in salvation today.

Let us read a number of passages in the Scriptures and I shall comment on them as we read.

One: the Conscience

"How much more shall the blood of Christ, who through the eternal Spirit offered himself without blemish unto God, cleanse your conscience from dead works to serve the living God?" (Heb. 9.14) This verse tells us to what degree Christ can save our conscience. His blood is able to cleanse it from dead works.

Let me ask you about your conscience? Is it under accusation? If yours is constantly under accusation, you have not fully possessed what Christ has accomplished for you. The Lord saves us; and His blood cleanses our conscience. It is so cleansed by His blood that there is no more condemnation. When we gather together we may sometimes pray, "O God, we thank You for we have our hearts sprinkled from an evil conscience"; yet afterwards we are frequently troubled. This that happens simply indicates that we have only had our conscience covered or that it is at times overlooked. But the blood of the Son of God is able to cleanse us. So that if our conscience is still under accusation, we have not received full salvation yet. This is not due to any inability of the salvation of God. Not at all. On the contrary, let us praise and thank Him that He is able to save us to the extent of having our conscience totally cleansed. Having our conscience completely cleansed *is* possible.

Two: the Heart

"For from within, out of the heart of men, evil thoughts proceed, fornications, thefts, murders, adulteries, covetings, wickednesses, deceit, lasciviousness, an evil eye, railing, pride, foolishness: all these evil things proceed from within, and defile the man" (Mark 7.21–23). "Blessed are the pure in heart: for they shall see God" (Matt. 5.8).

These two passages of Scripture show us the original defiled condition of our heart as well as the pureness in heart obtainable through the salvation of Christ.

The heart which Mark speaks of is our natural heart. What is the condition of that heart? "All these evil things proceed from within," says the Lord. Oh, how much wickedness comes out of the heart! But in Matthew's Gospel we find the Lord declaring: "Blessed are the pure in heart"—He is able to save the heart and change it from wickedness to pureness.

The way to have our heart saved is not by suppressing the evils within so that they will not come out; rather, it is by a cleansing from the inside out. If we attempt to cover or to seal up, let it be said that such is not salvation; because we have not yet been saved to the point of pureness of heart. We should in- quire before the Lord as to how much evil thoughts, craftiness, and pride we have in our hearts. If these be only suppressed within us, we merely cover them over and our hearts are still not saved. Does not God in fact say, "Blessed are the *pure in heart*" (Matt. 5.8)?

Our lack of testimony today is due to our hearts not being pure. How often we notice sin in people and yet we ourselves dare not reprimand: their outward action is but the flower of sin, yet in our own hearts we too have the seed for the same such flowering. Though we may not love the world like others, never- theless our hearts are somewhat affected too. There is not much difference between us and them. Without pureness of heart, there can be no testimony.

God will not leave any uncleanness in our heart. A heart as evil as is described by Mark may be delivered into purity. God can save us and give us a pure heart. Let us therefore thank and praise Him because He is able to save us to such an extent. He can transform a bad heart into a good and pure heart.

Three: All the Heart

"Thou shalt love the Lord thy God with *all* thy heart, and with *all* thy soul, and with *all* thy mind, and with *all* thy strength. The second is this, Thou shalt *love thy neighbor as thyself*" (Mark 12.30–31a). This verse tells us how God is able to save us so as to love Him with *all* our faculties and to love people with *total unselfishness.*

How difficult for us to love God to the degree of "all"! Frequently we think of loving Him as well as of loving the world secretly, of serving God as well as serving mammon. Time and again, many people and many things divide our hearts from loving God! Yet He is well able to save us to the magnitude of this "all"—enabling us to love Him with all our heart, all our soul, all our mind, and all our strength. And to save us, furthermore, to the extent of loving people without any heart of selfishness.

If today we are yet unable to love God to the degree of this all (having people or things or affairs as the focus of our love instead) and to love our neighbors as ourselves, we have not known the full salvation. Christ can save us so as to love God with such "allness" as well as to love our neighbors without selfishness. This *is* possible. Praise His name!

Four: the Mind

"But I fear, lest by any means, as the serpent beguiled Eve in his craftiness, your minds should be corrupted from the simplicity and the purity that is toward Christ" (2 Cor. 11.3). This passage shows us how our *minds* may be saved to the extent of utter *simplicity* and *purity.*

Oftentimes we find it very difficult to submit to the Lord and to love Him with singleness of mind. Indeed, this is most difficult. We just do not have such power. It is beyond us. How we long to love the Lord with perfect love and in simplicity, without any guile but in all purity. This, we agree, would be so good! This we hope, yet it seemingly is so unattainable. However, God is able to save us to that degree. It is not only possible but also attainable.

Our mind should be pure. If, however, we are double-minded, we will be like Eve. On the one hand Eve saw that the tree of the knowledge of good and evil was good for food but on the other hand reasoned that God had charged her not to eat of its fruit. She saw that the fruit was a delight to the eyes and much to be desired but also remembered that God had commanded that it not be eaten. Yet being so aroused, Eve ate of the forbidden fruit. Thus by deviating just a little, she lost the simplicity and purity that is towards the Lord.

Let us ask ourselves, Do we have the simplicity and purity of heart towards Christ? We need never be afraid of loving Him too much. We should love Him without any consideration and without any argument. Praise God, He can save us to such a place as that! It is quite possible to have a simple and pure heart towards the Lord.

"And be not fashioned according to this world: but be ye *transformed by the renewing of your mind*, that ye may prove what is the good and acceptable and perfect will of God" (Rom. 12.2). By this verse we are told once again that God is able to save our mind by renewing it to that place wherein it can prove what is the good and acceptable and perfect will of God.

Have you ever thought of this that has just been said? A renewed mind can actually prove what the good and acceptable and perfect will of God is. How frequently on a given point this thing seems to be God's will but that thing seems also to be His will. How often we mistake one for the other. But a *renewed* mind will make no mistake concerning the will of God. Unless our mind is renewed, we will not be able to prove what the will of God is. And thus we will not have experienced a full salvation. Yet God has not only saved us to where we are today, He will also save us even further to a perfect position. And it is to this that we must aspire and it is for this that we must thank God: because this too is attainable as well as possible.

Five: Our Thought

"Casting down *imaginations*, and every high thing that is exalted against the knowledge of God, and bringing every *thought* into captivity to the *obedience of Christ*; and being in readiness to avenge all disobedience, when your obedience shall be made full" (2 Cor. 10.5-6). These two verses show us that God can save our thought and bring it to the obedience of Christ.

Let each one of us ask this question: Am I able to control my own thoughts? How well we know that we fail to control many of our thoughts. Nonetheless, God enjoins us not to have a great many confused ideas. He will lead all these into captivity to the obedience of Christ.

May I inquire of you whether your thoughts are obedient to the Lord? It is not right for you to entertain wandering thoughts, unclean thoughts, and a secret desire for the world. If there are such thoughts as these, they are a sure indication that you have not yet obtained a full salvation. For the salvation of the Lord is well able to bring every thought of a believer to the obedience of Christ. This *is* attainable. We can commit all our thoughts and imaginations to Christ for them to be made to submit to Him. For this is according to the salvation prepared for us in Christ. God will not only save us to heaven by giving us eternal life, He will also save our entire being by leading all our thoughts to the obedience of Christ. Praise the Lord that this is not only possible but also attainable. He is able to save us to the uttermost.

"Wherefore *girding up the loins of your mind*, be sober and set your hope perfectly on the grace that is to be brought unto you at the revelation of Jesus Christ" (1 Peter 1.13). This word informs us that God is able to save our scattered thoughts to the point of concentration.

As most of us may know, the dress of the Jews in the olden days hung rather loosely on the body and was without any buttons. Each time a person started for work he had to gird up the loins so as to ease his movement. Our scattered thoughts are like ungirded loins. Yet God can gather up our scattered thoughts as a person girds up his loins.

How often our thoughts, though not unclean, are scattered and not focused. In prayer and in the study of God's word, our mind will run wild. Our thoughts may not be bad, but even good and tasteful thoughts are not conceived at the right time. This is because the loins of our mind are too loose and not concentrated. Yet God is well able to restrain our minds and bring our thoughts into focus. If our minds lack the power of concentration we have yet to experience the full salvation of the Lord. Thanks be to God, because He can deliver us from scattered thoughts and save us to the place of concentration. This is both possible and attainable.

Six: the Heart and Our Thought

"In nothing be anxious; but in everything by prayer and supplication with thanksgiving let your requests be made known unto God. And the peace of God, which passeth all understanding, shall guard your *hearts* and your *thoughts* in Christ Jesus" (Phil. 4.6–7).

The word "guard" here is a special military term. The better translation for it would be the verb "garrison"—which therefore gives this verse the following meaning: that the peace of God shall guard our hearts and thoughts just as, under martial law, gendarmes will garrison an area so effectively that it remains safe from any untoward incident. Think of it! The peace of God can garrison our hearts and thoughts in just such a manner: God is able to deliver us from all anxieties.

Seldom have I seen Christians without anxiety. The vast majority are weighed down with many worries. There was once a mother who had seven sons.

She declared, "I am worried to death about every son of mine until they all grow up to be saved. I do not need to worry for two of them because they have already gone to heaven. But I still have five sons to worry about." When a brother told her that it was wrong for her to worry—that it actually was a sin to worry—she retorted by saying, "A mother ought to be anxious for her own children. *Not* to worry is sinful." So this brother showed her the words in Philippians 4.6–7. Yet she regarded the anxiety spoken of there as probably not having reference to her kind of anxiety, for according to her thinking, a wife ought to worry about her husband, parents ought to worry about their children, and businessmen ought to be anxious about their business. Let us clearly see, though, that the Bible states categorically: "In *nothing* be anxious"—period!

Rarely have I ever met brothers or sisters who have not been worried about something. Such worry is not perfect salvation. If one is anxious about his family or is worried concerning everything around him, how will the peace of God ever be able to guard his heart and thought? Such a person cannot testify that his Lord bears his burden daily.

To be anxious is sin. God can deliver us from all anxieties. In matters both large and small, serious and light, there should not be any anxiety. If anyone has not experienced the garrisoning of his heart and thought by the peace of God, the salvation he has obtained is not yet complete. Were he clearly to understand the implication of such a verse, he would no doubt pray: "O Lord, of that which You have given me I have received too little!" Praise and thank God, He is able to deliver us from all anxieties so that we may live without any worry. His peace is well able to garrison our hearts and thoughts. This is something absolutely possible, for which we will continually praise Him.

Seven: the Mind to Suffer

"Forasmuch then as Christ *suffered* in the flesh, *arm* ye yourselves also with the same *mind*; for he that hath suffered in the flesh hath ceased from sin; that ye no longer should live the rest of your time in the flesh to the lusts of men, but to the will of God" (1 Peter 4.1-2). These two verses tell us how God is able to save our mind so that we shall be willing to suffer like Christ.

Are we afraid of suffering? We certainly are. How we long to spend each day comfortably and with no trial. Whenever a little hardship comes our way, we immediately ask God to remove it. During moments of true obedience to God we are threatened with the prospect of a hard and bitter future; and so we think of asking God to keep these unpleasantnesses from us. Nonetheless, God can save us to such an extent that we neither fear difficulty nor suffering. We are armed with the mind to suffer.

What kind of weapon is this? It is the best weapon: for it is to be armed with the same mind to suffer as Christ had. Whenever you are obedient to God you will be told by people how hard your life will be and how cruel men will treat you. Yet in response you will think of Christ, of how he suffered in the flesh, and that therefore you too must suffer. This is the way for you to be armed: I come to suffer. Suffering is not only my duty but it is also my office. Suffering is my business and I embrace it most willingly. Armed with such a weapon as this, you can defeat anything. Not a being afraid to suffer, but on the contrary a welcoming of it. Not that you draw back in the face of suffering, but that you let it find you. If you are afraid when you think of suffering and try to escape, the salvation you have experienced is not yet complete. For God is able to save you by giving you a mind to suffer. Only thus are you able to "live the rest of your time in the flesh to the will of God"—Thank and praise God, this is possible!

Eight: the Tongue

"If any man thinketh himself to be religious, while he *bridleth not his tongue* but deceiveth his heart, this man's religion is vain. Pure religion and undefiled before our God and Father is this, to visit the fatherless and widows in their affliction, and to keep oneself unspotted from the world" (James 1.26–27). "*But the tongue can no man tame*; it is a restless evil, it is full of deadly poison. Therewith bless we the Lord and Father; and therewith curse we men, who are made after the likeness of God: out of the same mouth cometh forth blessing and cursing. My brethren, these things ought not so to be" (James 3.8–10).

These two Bible passages reveal how no man can

tame the tongue. Yet God is able to save this untamable member of ours and keep it bridled.

Once I met a person who said, "Since James clearly states that no man can tame the tongue, it is therefore excusable for a Christian not to bridle his tongue." What we should know is that James also declares emphatically in the same passage: "*These things ought not so to be*" (v.10). Moses was unable to enter Canaan because of one reason, which was that "he spake unadvisedly with his lips" (Ps. 106.33). He spoke as though he were uninstructed. In order to know how to speak, we need "the tongue of the instructed" (Is. 50.4 Darby) as well as the ears of the instructed. God can save not only our heart, thought and mind to perfection but also our tongue. If we cannot control it, I say again that we are not the possessors of a perfect salvation. Let God be praised, He is able to save our tongue whole. This is not only possible, it is also attainable.

Nine: Fleshly Lusts

"So then, brethren, we are *debtors, not to the flesh*, to live after the flesh" (Rom. 8.12). This verse tells us that God is quite able to save us from the natural demands of the flesh and to overcome all fleshly lusts.

Here I would particularly mention the three basic drives or instincts of our human body (the flesh): (1) to be nourished for the sake of living; (2) to reproduce itself for the sake of extending the human race, and (3) to be protected for the sake of preserving itself. Before the fall, these three matters were perfectly proper, for there was no sin mixed in with them. But after man had sinned, sin found its way into all three, thus making them the catalysts for subsequent sinning.

Seizing upon this need for bodily nourishment, the world as a system has ever since used food and drink to tempt us. The primal temptation to man lies in this very matter of nourishment. As the fruit of the tree of the knowledge of good and evil was used by the enemy to tempt Eve, so the excessive feasting of today becomes a fleshly sin. Let us not overlook this matter of eating, because many carnal believers fail in this very point. Because of food, the carnal Christian in Corinth stumbled many brethren (see 1 Cor. 8). Hence no one could become an elder or deacon in the early church unless he had overcome in the matter of eating and drinking (see 1 Tim. 3.3 mg.,8).

In the area of reproduction, let us note that after the fall of man it too had the capacity to degenerate into human passion and lust. Lust and human flesh are especially connected in the Scriptures. Note that in the Garden of Eden the sin of greediness instantly aroused lust and brought on shame. In his first letter to the Corinthians Paul puts these two things together (6.13). He also connects drunkards with the covetous (vv.9–10).

Finally, there is man's instinct for self-preservation. After sin had begun to rule over man, physical strength began to be engaged for self-protection. So that everything which today stands in the way of our enjoyment and comfort is to be opposed. The so-called bad temper and its fruit of anger and strife emanate from the flesh and are sins of the flesh. In the name of self-preservation many sins are committed both directly and indirectly as motivated by the sin principle operating within us. To protect our own interests, to preserve our own existence, to propel our own fame, and to promote our own ideas, mankind has given the world many of the darkest sins ever seen.

If we analyze the many sins of the world, we shall see how much they are related to these three drives or instincts of the body as they have been misused by man. And a carnal Christian is one who is under the control of all three or any one of these three misused urges of the body.

Now Paul declares that we are no longer debtors to the flesh. We do not owe the flesh anything, he says. Every one of us may live without obeying the flesh. Christ is able to deliver us from all lustful passions and desires. What is lust? We human beings have two urges: (1) a set of natural demands, and (2) another kind of urge that arises out of these same natural demands—the urge to use improper means to satisfy these natural demands. Now this second urge is what is called a fleshly lust. But our Lord Jesus Christ can deliver us from such fleshly lusts.

The Lord is able to save us to the point of our giving *no ground* to any fleshly lust. He is also able to save us to the position of even overcoming all natural desires. Yet let us not proceed from this to make the mistake of thinking that Christ will deliver us from *having* any natural desire, for this is unwarranted from Scripture. What the Bible says is only that Christ is able to make us *overcome* our natural desires. The Scriptures never teach that the flesh will disappear. It only affirms that we believers are no longer debtors to the flesh, and that therefore we have no obligation to fulfill the natural demands of the flesh. True, whatever is owed must be repaid; but now owing nothing, we are therefore able to control ourselves.

For instance, when a person is hungry he wishes to eat. This is one of man's natural desires. But if he has no money to buy food and he begins to use an improper method (such as stealing money for food) to satisfy his natural desire,* this turns to be a gratification not of a natural desire but of a fleshly lust. Man is only to use ways to satisfy his natural desires which are according to the Scriptures. If he is hungry and has money, he can buy food to eat. And this is not sinful. All natural desires must be met by means which are according to the teaching of God. Any deviation turns the natural desire into a fleshly lust. Bu God enables us to overcome natural desires and to be delivered from fleshly lusts. Hence it means that when we are hungry and *without* money, we can overcome the craving of hunger and refuse to use improper means for its satisfaction.* Hungering is unavoidable, but there is to be no hankering after fleshly lusts.

The same rule applies to reproduction and preser-

---

*For more on this kind of situation, see the third paragraph below.—*Translator*

vation. Everything to do with natural desire in these two areas must be done only in accordance with the teachings of the Bible. Whatever goes beyond natural desire within the Biblical context is sin. We do have natural desires which are not sinful in themselves. However, we are not debtors to the flesh, we have no obligation to repay it. So that in both of these areas, God is able to save us—delivering us from the demands of fleshly lusts and enabling us when necessary to overcome natural desire.

Our being not debtors to the flesh implies much more here. Even when we are sick, we owe nothing to the flesh. Our nerves may be feeble, yet we need not lose our temper. In spite of physical or psychological deficiency, we may still overcome. The word of God tells us that we are not debtors to the flesh. Can it be that because of imperfection in a certain part of a believer's make-up, God is not able to save a Christian to the uttermost? Far be such a thought. Let us continually remind ourselves that we owe *nothing* to the flesh.

May I ask you, Are you seized with a certain physical difficulty? Are you bound by some problem regarding eating and drinking? Then you ought to know that the salvation of the Lord is equal to all circumstances and problems. For as your difficulties are, so is the salvation of Christ. Suppose a Christian is in hunger for one day, two days, even three days. Can you tell him that he must not steal to gratify the craving of his hunger? You must. Is it all right for him to be a thief because he is hungry? Not so, for there is no situation wherein a Christian need be forced to sin. God can save every one of us who does not live according to the flesh. "Knowing this, that our old man was crucified with him, that the body of sin might be done away, that so we should no longer be in bondage to sin" (Rom. 6.6). Consequently, let us stand before God and say to Him: "God, I thank You, for whatever is in my old man was crucified with Christ on the cross! Be it jealousy, pride, unclean thoughts, a wandering mind, worry, or fleshly lusts—Christ can deliver me from all these. Praise the Lord!"

Ten: Our Bodily Members

"Neither present your members unto sin as instruments of unrighteousness; but present yourselves unto God, as alive from the dead, and your *members as instruments of righteousness unto God*" (Rom. 6.13). "I speak after the manner of men because of the infirmity of your flesh: for as ye presented your members as servants to uncleanness and to iniquity unto iniquity, even so now *present your members as servants to righteousness unto sanctification*" (Rom. 6.19).

These two passages show us how God is able to save our bodily members to sanctification.

Formerly our members served as servants to sin, they being given over to uncleanness and iniquity How about now? Have we been delivered from the sins of all the members of our body? Have we presented our members to be servants to righteousness? If we have not presented them as such, then we are still serving sin and have not yet obtained full salvation. But Christ can save all the members of our body to be servants to righteousness toward sanctification. This is possible and attainable. Praise His name!

Eleven: the I

"*I have been* crucified with Christ; and it is no longer I that live, but *Christ liveth in me*: and that life which I now live in the flesh I live in faith, the faith which is in the son of God, who loved me, and gave himself up for me" (Gal. 2.20).

This is a scripture verse with which we are most familiar and which many of us can recite by memory. This word declares that God saves us to the extent that we were not only crucified with Christ but now Christ lives in us.

The word here is not that we may be like Christ or that we must imitate Christ; but rather, it says Christ now lives in us. Thus had God saved Paul, and in like manner will He save us.

If we have not yet experienced Christ living in us, the salvation which we know is still incomplete. Thanks be to God that He saves us to the place where *for me to live is Christ*. This is possible and attainable by all Christians.

There is one thing which we must pay special attention to, which is, that the full salvation which God has prepared for us must be received in full. I do not believe in sinless perfection—in the eradication of the root of sin; but I do believe God is able to save me to the uttermost. I do not believe the cross annihilates me, yet I do believe that there my Lord has died for me. Not that God has pulled out the root of my sin, but that He gives me a Christ to live in me. Formerly Christ died on the cross for me; now He lives in me and for me. The sphere of God's salvation is the sphere of my redemption. There is no need for us to retain ill-temper, uncleanness, anxiety, or fleshly lusts. God is able to deliver us from all of them. He not only saves us from the bad but also gives us the good.

In this present discussion, then, we have come to see how immense is God's salvation! How great is the sphere of our salvation! It is as if the goods have already been selected; now then, how are we going to acquire them? We know we must pay the price. And in our next discussion to follow we will speak on this matter of the price to be paid.* But here I would like for you to do one thing: I would invite you to *believe in God's word*. Since the word of God tells us He is able to save us so completely, you will have His full salvation if you only believe. We ought to believe that all these things pertaining to His salvation are possible. The greatest problem lies in the fact that we cannot believe what the Bible says. For God will *fulfill* His word according to your *faith*. But we will have not if we believe not.

How serious this is! God's word has already been spoken! And if you say possible, it is possible; but if

---

*See the next chapter.—*Translator*

you say impossible, it will be impossible. You must believe in God's word, and then shall He perform it for you according to your faith.

Andrew Murray was a deeply spiritual Christian. I read his writings with special care. And I find that each time he speaks on the life that wins or on the holy life or the restful life, he always gives readers a few conditions. Among them all is to be found one common factor: *that people must believe that such and such is possible*. Indeed, if men consider anything to be impossible, God is unable to perform it for them. Whereas if men believe that God has said so and that He is able to do it for them, God will fulfill in them what He says.

Inquire of yourself as to what you think of your Christian life. If you must confess that your current situation is very much deficient, then do you wish God to bring His full salvation to you? If you really *want* God's full salvation, then *believe* this is possible and obtainable. Allow Him to fulfill His work in you.

2 | The Life That Wins

We have already seen in the preceding chapter that a Christian life may attain to full salvation, that a believer may have a clear conscience and a clean heart and may be without anxiety and possess a pure and concentrated mind. He is able to overcome all physical defects and to present the members of his body to God as instruments of righteousness to sanctification. Every Christian may arrive at the place where he can honestly say: I am crucified with Christ, and it is no longer I who lives but Christ who lives in me. All these things are not only possible but also attainable. Now, though, we need to discuss how we obtain this life that wins.

One: What Kind of Life Christ Lived on Earth

We know that when Christ lived on earth He wholly obeyed God, not loving the world at all nor following His own will in words and deeds for a single moment. He never allowed temptation to overcome Him. He never sinned at any time but was obedient to God even to death. Such was the life of Christ on earth.

What about us who are Christ's followers? Have we obeyed God wholly? No, we have not. Can we say we have not followed our own will, not even in one instance? Impossible. Have we been able not to sin? Oh, we have committed many sins. Have we abstained from loving the world—not even loving it a little? We may not love it outwardly, but I am afraid that in our hearts we secretly love it. Who among us is not moved by temptation? There is none. Yet how can all these be true in our lives? For according to what the Bible says, a Christian ought to obey God entirely—not love the world, neither follow his own will nor sin nor be moved by any temptation. But do I not hear you say that this is impossible!?! I too say it is impossible! Many of us have been Christians for at least a year or two; and most of us have been Christians for three, five, or even more years. During these years, how much have we accomplished? How many times have we sorrowfully had to repent, even to the point of weeping? Where, then, is the victory?

We truly know the standard laid down in the Bible for a Christian. We as followers of Christ must not follow our own will but be righteous as God is righteous and seek with singleness of heart His kingdom. But are we really such in actuality? How frequently we sin. How often our heart is unclean, our temper often flares up. We surreptitiously love the world and are controlled by fleshly lusts. We do not love the Bible, nor do we desire to pray. And sometimes we are tempted to say that it is better for us not to be a Christian.

Alas, the Bible says we *ought*; and yet we say we *cannot*. Can we not ask God to lower His truth a little? Can He not agree with us that it is not serious to sin once in a while? Can it not be argued that some people may be able to love and obey God, to deny self and to be holy, but such a standard is for a special class of people and not for me?

What we as believers see is that even if we cannot, there *is* One who can, and that One is Christ. We know we ought to be perfect, yet we cannot be. Nonetheless, Christ has already done it, and thus He is perfect. Here we come to know three things:

1. that there is a living standard which God has set for every Christian to live by;

2. that we are nonetheless unable to live by it; and

3. that throughout the centuries there has only been One who has so lived, who is Christ.

In other words we ought but we cannot. Yet at the same time we acknowledge that Christ has already attained perfection. And hence all this demonstrates the fact that *only God himself can live up to the living standard He has established*. Put another way, we may say that it takes the same life to live the comparable kind of living. For example, only a bird can live a bird's life or an animal live an animal's life. So that it may accurately be stated that only God can live God's life. And since Christ is God, therefore Christ alone can live God's type of living.

Two: What the Bible Says about the Christian Life

"For to me to live is Christ" (Phil. 1.21). Does this verse say *like* Christ? No. Does it say *imitate* Christ? Again, No. Does it say taking Christ as the *model* and following Him? No once again. It says that for me to live *is* Christ. It is absolutely impossible to imitate, and it is completely useless trying to be good. Even though we are able to read the Bible and pray and live a good life, if our life is wrong, our living will likewise be wrong. Nothing is wrong with our aspiring, weeping, and repenting before God and saying, "O God, I really want to obey You"—no, what is wrong with us is simply that our life is wrong.

God not only appoints Christ to die at Calvary for us but also makes Him our life. Do be very clear about this: God does not make you a Christian in the way a person teaches a monkey how to dress, eat, and move. To teach a monkey to live like a man would be such a burden to it that it would rather remain as it is than learn to be a man. No, God has not treated us in such a way.

We may read the Bible for five minutes and find it tasteless, yet in reading other books we have much more interest. We may pray and get nothing; and yet, if we do not pray, our conscience will accuse us. We cannot help ourselves from loving the world; nevertheless, in loving the world we do not have peace within. It is extremely difficult to be a Christian. How impossible it is to live a God-like life. We are truly most wretched! Let me add, though, that as long as we feel wretched there is still hope because such wretched feeling is proof that we are still on the way. If a person no longer feels wretched, I must feel wretched for him because he has already left the straight path.

Oftentimes we are left speechless as we witness the severity of the temptations of this world. How can we therefore blame other people when we too are moved within? Frequently we long to be like others who are so obedient to God in showing their back to the world and turning their face to Him. We ourselves have tried and have found how difficult it is. And how miserable we have become as we have sought to be a Christian like this! For who is able to achieve so high a standard? Is not such expectation much like asking a five-year-old child to carry 300 pounds? Oh how cruel! And it would obviously be extremely brutal to force such a child to carry 10,000 pounds. Yet to ask a Christian to live a God-like life is far more wretched than asking a five-year-old to carry 10,000 or even 300 pounds.

Very often, however, we do try to measure up to such a life. We admire such a walk and we are willing to suffer for it. But what happens is that before one sin is cleared up, another has appeared on the scene. Or else before we have finished our repentance for one thing, the very same thing has occurred once again. Before our repentant tears have even dried, the woeful thing has returned to haunt us.

Oh, let me say that if only we could truly believe that "we cannot"—how much better it would be! God does not want you to try. The life which He gives us is not a fall-and-repent type of life. He wants us to live as Christ lives; because it is Christ in us who wishes to live out His style of life.

Mary gave the Lord a body through which He could exhibit a God-like life. In like manner, if we give ourselves to the Lord and accept this Christ, God will cause us to live out the life which Christ himself once lived.

Please note carefully that to be holy and not follow your own will, to love the Lord with singleness of heart and obey Him entirely is not something you can try to do or to imitate. It depends completely on the Christ whom God has provided for us. And this is full salvation. God has provided Christ for two purposes: on the one hand Christ keeps the law for us, on the other hand He lives in us so that we too may keep the law of God. On the one hand He died for us, on the other hand He lives in us. At Calvary He accomplished salvation for us; now He implements that accomplishment in us. At Calvary He justified us; dwelling in us He now makes us righteous. Not only did *He* obey God, but by living in us He causes *us* to obey God too. He not only did everything *for* us; He also does all things *in* us.

Here we may perceive the significance of *resurrection*. "If Christ hath not been raised," declared Paul, "ye are yet in your sins" (1 Cor. 15.17). Do notice that the apostle does not say here that the matter of sin yet remains, since by the *death* of Christ the legal case of sin has been dismissed before God; but he does say that if Christ has not been *raised* from the dead, we are yet in our sins; and therefore we will only receive half the salvation of the Lord. In preaching the gospel we often use a parable such as this: we who have sinned are like people in debt, Christ is like a rich friend, and in His death as our friend He pays off our debt. Now no doubt this is good news, yet unfortunately this is but half a salvation. Yes indeed, the Lord Jesus has paid off all the debts we owed. But we would ask if He *only* pays our debts. If so, can such limited action guarantee us never again to incur debt hereafter? Will we not go into debt again if Christ has merely paid off the old debt? It is most true that our friend has paid off what we owed before; nevertheless, after a while we shall again contract a debt for which our friend will need to pay again. Does not all this betray the fact that if Christ has only died for our sins, what we have received is but half a salvation? Though any earthly friend may have paid a debt for us, we can still continue to incur debt later on. Though Christ our heavenly friend has died for us, we will yet be in sins. Can the salvation of God ever be like this?

God's salvation causes the Lord Jesus to live in us as well as to die at Calvary for us. He not only pays all our debts but also lives in us so that we will never have to run into debt again. God does not save us merely to escape hell and to enter heaven: He saves us to the extent of Christ being our life. If you have only received half a salvation, you will doubtless be miserable and fail to experience the full joy of salvation. Jesus

Christ is our life to do everything in us. God never demands Christians to *do* this or to *do* that. For Paul says, "For to me to live is Christ"—and having Christ living in him, Paul is able to endure beatings, persecutions, many perils, imprisonment in Jerusalem, and transference to Rome. It is not by his being like Christ nor imitating Christ, but by Christ living in him that he finds strength for all such things. As a monkey cannot be transformed into a man, so a Christian cannot imitate Christ.

". . . Work out your own salvation with fear and trembling; for it is God who worketh in you both to will and to work, for his good pleasure" (Phil. 2.12b–13). Chapter 1 and verse 21 of Philippians speaks of Paul's personal experience; these two verses from chapter 2 show what every Christian may experience.

"Work out your own salvation with fear and trembling"—Many who read these words surmise that *they* must work out their own salvation. And so they decide to rise early, to read the Bible, and to witness with great zeal. Surprisingly they find they cannot do these things. This is because they overlook the words of the next clause which says: "for it is God who worketh in you both to will and to work" (v.13). The very word "for" indicates this to be a "cause"; whereas, what verse 12 says about working out your own salvation is but an "effect".

What we ordinarily do in our daily life consists mainly of the following two things: (1) to will, which is an inward decision; and (2) to work, which is an outward act. Without question, these two things sum up our life. We plan within and act without. But both to will and to work are the results of God's prior working in us. The Scripture here does not say that you should will and work; it says instead that it is *God who works in you* both to will and work. God first works in you, thus enabling you to will and to work. Because God has worked in, therefore you can work out. Without the first working, there cannot be the second.

Time and again we plead with God, saying: "O God, I wish to obey You wholly, but I find it is most difficult. I do not want to love the world, but how hard it is. I do not desire to follow myself, but it seems impossible not to do so." Yet here is the kind of salvation which is presented to us: that God is able to work in us and make us obey Him wholly, to not love the world and to not follow our own selves. Though in ourselves we cannot, God may so work in us that we can.

What is full salvation? It does not mean that a Christian gets rid of one sin today and another one tomorrow. A full salvation means accepting a *full Christ*. And having such a Christ, we have full salvation. The most difficult Christian to be helped is one whose eyes do not see Christ. What he sees is either his own good or his own bad. His attention is focused on a certain sin of his, or the harassment that may be inflicted upon him by certain people, or the attraction of a particular thing. For this he bemoans himself and hates himself, thinking of ways to overcome. This is a big mistake, however, for God has not called us to overcome one thing after another nor to perform one good act after another; instead, He asks us to accept a full Christ.

For example, a child loves fruit. Today he thinks of eating pears; so he goes to the orchard to buy some. Tomorrow he wishes to eat an apple or a peach, and so he will go again to buy some apples or peaches. Later on he finds out that his father is the owner of this orchard, and that he also gives this orchard to him. Thereafter, the whole situation is changed, since now all these fruits belong to him. Similarly, we Christians think of doing one thing today and another thing the next day. Today we need patience, tomorrow we need love. We are like this child who buys pears today and apples or peaches tomorrow. Yet God invites us to accept a full Christ: God's entire "spiritual" orchard now belongs to us, even a full Christ. But in buying according to retail, one has to go buy again and again whenever he is in lack.

I do not say here that you and I do not need patience or love. We must certainly exhibit these virtues. Yet how impossible it is to do one thing after another. For if you try and try, you will find yourself loving the world more, becoming prouder, and increasingly following your own will as the days go by. You ought to know that the entire "orchard" is yours. God wants you to share one goal, which is, to possess a full Christ. Christ in you and me will enable us to will and to work for God's good pleasure.

You may have heard the truth of Christ living His life in us before, but I want to ask you if you have possessed this truth in experience? How often we know, and though we try, we still fail.

"But of him are ye in Christ Jesus, who was made unto us wisdom from God, both righteousness and sanctification and redemption" (1 Cor. 1.30 mg.). If we read this verse most carefully and slowly we can readily see that at the time we are saved God has made Christ to be our personal righteousness and our personal sanctification. The answer is Christ. What is victory? It is Christ. What are patience and humility? They are Christ. Anyone who is able to answer in this way has found the secret. My whole being is corrupt and fleshly; but Christ is my holiness. He is my sanctification. There is no one who is holy and victorious; even so, there is a way in which we can say to God, "O God, I accept your Son!" And that will be our holiness and that will be our victory.

Three: When It Is That Christ Lives in Me

If it is true that Christ alone has the life that wins, then when does He begin to live in us? Let us recognize that at the time we are saved we possess Christ. "He that *hath the Son hath the life*" (1 John 5.12). "But as many as *received him*, to them gave he the right to become children of God, even to them that believe on his name" (John 1.12). When we believe, we already have Christ. "Or know ye not as to your own selves, that Jesus Christ is in you? unless indeed ye be reprobate" (2 Cor. 13.5a). Who are those who are not considered reprobate by the Lord?

"And him that cometh to me I will in no wise cast out" (John 6.37b). Have you come to the Lord? If we have come to Him we are not reprobates. What, then, do we have? We have Jesus Christ in us. For this reason it is a serious blunder for anyone to tell you that though you have believed on the Lord, you do not have Christ in you. If you are not saved, you must receive Christ; but if you are saved, He *is already in you.*

Four: How to Let Christ Live Out His Life in Me

Now we know that only Christ is victorious. We also know that He lives in us. For when we believe in Him, we have Him. Yet day by day I am still myself as though nothing had happened. What should we do in order that Christ may live out His life in us? There are two ways, or may we say that there are two conditions.

First, *surrender.* Yes, Christ is indeed in me, but He cannot do anything if I do not let Him. You and I must obey God. What precisely is surrender? Surrender is not a promising God to do His will, nor is it *making covenant* with God to do what cannot be done. To surrender is for me *to take my hands off my own life.* It is to give over into God's hand my good and bad, my strength and weakness, my past and future, my very life and very self so that God alone may work in me.

If we do not remove our hands from off our lives, God has no way to live out His life through us. Suppose you give a book to someone, yet your hand will not let loose of the book; will your friend be able to receive it? When we come to God we must say to Him, "I hand over to You all my good and bad, my likes and dislikes, my willing and not willing, my do's and do not's." Are we willing to do this? If we are not, there is nothing God can do for us. It is our responsibility to hand over our defeated selves. God is ever ready, waiting for you and me to do this one thing, to be willing to hand over these selves of ours.

This condition of surrender is not the asking of us to do what we cannot do. It only requires us to hand over our good and bad, our strength and weakness, even our all. Once I read a story about a young man who declared that he was willing for everything except for one matter. Which was, that if God were to ask him to preach to the Catholic people he was determined he would not go. Oh, let me ask, Are you willing to hand over an unwilling heart to the Lord?

Surrender involves two aspects: one is to offer to be used of God, the other is to offer to let God do His work. Yet how many there are who think of surrender only in terms of offering themselves to be used of God and neglect this other aspect. Actually, God asks you to do but one thing really, which is to give yourself to Him from this point on. And such giving constitutes a dying to self. It is a being delivered from your own flesh. You must hand over yourself. Are you willing to do this? It is well if you do.

How very hard it is for you to take your hand off the person or the thing that you love. I say it is most difficult. For you feel you have to pay such a high price and are therefore most reluctant to let go. For instance, you know you are often defeated in the matter of friendship. It is very hard for you to say to God, "Whether my friends are good or bad, I give them all to You. I ask You to deliver me." Or let me use another example. If you pray for someone in whom you do not have any deep interest, you can easily believe that God will help him. And whether or not he *is* helped or healed poses no problem to you. But let your parent or wife or husband or very close friend be sick, and you will discover how hard it is to commit him or her to God. For if he or she is *not* helped or healed, you are afraid that that one may die. This proves that the more you love, the less easy to let go your hand.

What God requires today is not how much good you must do. He only asks you to hand over your all to Him. We encounter so much defeat in our lives as to discourage us. Until a few months ago, I had a sin which I could not overcome. And I did not have the faith to commit it to God. Once, twice, many times I tried to overcome, but nothing happened. At last I was able to hand it over to God. Hence the question today lies in whether or not you are willing to put yourself entirely in the hand of God. Irrespective of people, the world, sin, or whatever, if you find you in your own strength cannot let them go, then realize that you can overcome if you are willing to tell God, "O God, I commit to You what I cannot let go of. Please work in me till I am willing to let go."

Let me say to you that I am not afraid if you cannot let go, neither am I afraid if your weakness should increase a hundredfold nor if you commit more sins: I am only fearful that you are not willing to hand over yourself to God for Him to work in you. Are you willing to hand over to Him that person or friend whom you love, that special sin of yours, some particular problem which has ceaselessly plagued you, or those things which displease Him? The crux of the matter lies not in the tens of thousands of weaknesses and defeats you have but in whether you are willing to say to God, "O God, I hand over my all to You."

This act of surrender is not meant to make you suffer; it instead is meant to express your desire of letting God work in you till you are perfectly willing to let go.

To surrender does not require you to do what you cannot do. It simply requires of you to put yourself in God's hand and let Him work until you are ready to obey Him and are willing to let all things go. If you are willing, God then has a way; for He is not frightened by the immensity of sin or the depravity of men: He is only dismayed at the failure of men to put their hearts in His hand.

To sum up, then, surrender means the yielding up of our will, which is to put ourselves in God's hand and let Him work till He is well-pleased.

The second way or condition for Christ to be able to live out His life in us is *to believe*. Since we have surrendered, we must now believe that God will deliver us from what we love, what we cannot and will not give up. "Commit thy way unto Jehovah; trust also in him, and he will bring it to pass" (Ps. 37.5). To commit is to surrender; to trust is to believe. And the result is that "he will bring it to pass." Knowing that we have no way, we commit ourselves to God and believe that the Lord who dwells in us will accomplish the work.

Can you say, I am victorious? Hallelujah, I can say I am victorious, because the Bible tells me so. How pitiful that our faith is less than the size of a grain of mustard—nay, even less than a speck of dust! If we have faith, God will begin to work. When the Lord created the heavens and the earth He merely used His mouth, for when He said "Let there be light" there was light! If we have faith, He most certainly will begin to work because He is anxious to have His work done.

Several weeks ago a brother came to talk with me. He said he had three or four sins which he could not overcome; hence he sometimes felt like committing suicide. "Do you believe Christ can deliver you from your sin?" I asked. "I do," he answered, "but I keep sinning again and again. Other sins I have overcome, but these few still remain." So I read with him Romans 8: "There is therefore now no condemnation to them that are in Christ Jesus" (v.1). I explained to him by saying, "Here in the Bible we are told of one condition for deliverance, which is for us to be in Christ Jesus. Are you in Christ Jesus?" "Yes," he answered, "I am in Christ Jesus." "Then look at what the Bible says," I responded; and I read to him this next passage from verse 2 ("For the law of the Spirit of life in Christ Jesus *made me free* from the law of sin and of death"). "The Bible says I am freed from the law of sin and of death. Are you now delivered?" I asked. "I dare not say that," he replied. "Then where is your faith?" I concluded.

I say again that I am not afraid of man's weakness, corruption, and sinfulness; no, I am fearful of only one kind of people—those who do not believe God's word. How precious are the words "made me free"! The word of God says "made me free" and not "going to make me free": Do we really believe this?

Christ has died for you. If you simply believe, you have eternal life. What proof do you have of this? Because the Bible says so. But note that the Bible also declares that "the law of the Spirit of life in Christ Jesus *made me free* from the law of sin and of death"—therefore, I am already freed, I have been delivered from the law of sin and of death. Even if there are hundreds, thousands, yea, tens of thousands of sins, I have been delivered from them all! I am delivered even from the spiritual death in Adam.

Do you believe in such a word? Do you believe you have already been delivered from the law of sin and of death? The Bible declares that you were made free. If you truly believe, you will shout, "Hallelujah, praise God! I am free from the law of sin and of death because the word of God says so!" Do you have any particular sin or some unclean thought which you cannot overcome? If so, know and realize that a gospel is preached to you today which declares that the law of the Spirit of life in Christ Jesus has made you free from such sin.

We need to see that surrender and faith are intimately related. When these two actions are joined

together, there is victory and no defeat. We will have
no victory if we merely believe and yet are unwilling
to give our lives to God in exchange for the life of
Christ. Though at the time of regeneration we have
already come into possession of this life of Christ,
God *will not force* us to live by the life of Christ if our
will is not surrendered to God to *let* Christ live in and
out through us. And by the same token, if we only
surrender but do not believe, such surrender will be
reduced to a kind of dead work; for although we are
prepared to give God *the right to work*, we have not
given Him the *opportunity to come in*.

Hence we must (1) lift up our head to look to God
and say, I hand over my all to You, I am willing to let
You work; and (2) believe that God has already
worked according to His word.

Christ has taken care of all the conflicts, for the
divine government is upon His shoulders. Let us
believe Him day by day, because faith needs to be
continued whereas surrender is done once and for all.
We may surrender to God in one instant and need
never do it again (Though some people surrender
gradually and slowly, this is unnecessary.). Having
committed ourselves to God in surrender, we believe
He will cause Christ to live His holiness and victory in
and through us. Formerly we were saved from the
punishment of hell; now we are saved from the power
of sin. Nothing needs to be done except surrender and
believe. May we prove that we are truly victorious.

It is quite simple: only believe. *Without* faith,
nothing avails; but *with* faith, there will be transfor-
mation. For God has said it. Let us praise and thank

Him! Let us believe with bare faith, not depending on feelings. Whatever God says, it is so. We have not seen heaven and hell, yet we believe in heaven and hell because of the word of God. Believing, we require no evidence. We need just one proof, and that is the word of God. Not because we see are we changed, but because we believe what the Lord has said. Believing, we change; not believing, we do not change.

Once I asked a brother if he believed Romans 8.2. He answered yes. So I pursued the matter further by asking that if he should get up tomorrow morning and commit the same sin again what would he do? He did not know how to answer. Let me observe that the greatest danger lies in the *first and basic temptation*. For Satan will suggest that surrender and belief are all in vain because you have sinned again. Wherein are you different from what you were before? he will ask. Are you not the same? But I say once and again that faith is *long-lived*. That which is short-lived is no faith. Of all which lives in the world, faith lives the longest. Temptation may come, but God says we are more than conquerors. We therefore will overcome, and temptation will fail. The way we deal with this basic temptation reveals whether or not we have true faith.

The Lord Jesus on one occasion said to His disciples, "Let us go over unto the other side" of the Lake of Galilee; but suddenly there arose a great storm, with the waves beating into the boat so much that it was beginning to fill up. The disciples therefore awakened the sleeping Jesus and cried, "Teacher, carest thou not that we perish?" Whereupon He arose and rebuked the wind and the storm. And the wind ceased, and there was a great calm. But then the Lord rebuked the disciples by saying, "Have ye not yet faith?" (Mark 4.35–40) Do let us see that since the Lord had commanded that they all go to the other side, the disciples and Jesus *would* get to the other side. The wind might blow harder and the waves might rise higher; yet nothing could hinder them from reaching the other shore because the Lord had said otherwise. Accordingly, what is of utmost importance is to *believe God's word*. If God says so, then *that* is enough; and nothing else matters.

3 | Living by Faith (A Talk to Young Christians)

My righteous one shall live by faith. (Heb. 10.38)

I have met many believers and often discussed with them various spiritual problems. Among these many problems, one difficulty appears to be the common lot of most people, and which many find it hard to overcome. Why is it that sometimes their spiritual life seems to be dry and spiritless while at other times it appears joyous and excited? Although they may not have a "third heaven" experience, they nonetheless have had what could be termed a mountain-top experience. They wonder how they can overcome the dry spells and maintain themselves in a continuously joyful and inspired position. How they would like to expect a life lived in a constant flow and even an overflowing state. And thus would they be able to sing hallelujahs throughout their lifetime. Such, then, is the problem which many believers desire to solve.

This kind of life that vacillates between dryness
and joy is what is commonly called by believers a
wave-like life or an up-and-down spiritual existence.
So far as their feeling goes, many Christians live at
times on the mountain tops and at other times in the
deep valleys. Sometimes they are tossed about by the
waves and sometimes they walk on the water.
Sometimes they are high, sometimes they are low.

Almost all Christians are conscious of their lives
being invaded by sudden ups-and-downs. On certain
days they feel so joyous that they could pray for
hours without the slightest weariness. When they
witness for the Lord, they could talk without ceas-
ing. The more they talk the more they *can* talk. If
they are hearing the word of God, they find it so in-
teresting that they could go on listening endlessly. Or
if they are reading the Bible, the taste of it is so
sweet—even like honey. On other days, though,
everything appears to have changed for the worse.
They cannot detect any difference between praying
and not praying. They find the reading of the Bible
dry and tasteless as though it were but black ink on
white paper. When they meet people they feel uneasy
if they do not testify; and hence they force
themselves to say a few words, such as "Believe in
the Lord Jesus and you will have eternal life"—but
in their hearts they sense such deadness as though
there were really nothing to say after all. During such
an arid period, all things are done by compulsion.
They do not experience any joy in drawing near to
God, and yet they know they must come to Him.

With the result that they force themselves to approach the Lord.

This kind of Christian life seems to find its counterpart in the natural realm. If there is a mountain peak, there must also be a deep valley. After the stormy waves there will be a calm surface. Having become accustomed to such experiences, many Christians conclude that it is impossible for believers to overcome such a vacillating existence and achieve a quiet and confident spiritual state. We are destined, such Christians believe, for such up-and-down experiences throughout our lives. Yet there is another group of Christians who declare that we need not lead such a peak-and-valley existence but that the Christian experience may very well be firm and as steady as a straight line. Let me suggest, however, that neither the Christian who leads an up-and-down life nor the believer who expects to have a straightforward experience is a hundred percent correct.

If we wish to find out the principle in a certain matter, we must first gather together the spiritual experiences of various groups of people and then try to discover a rule which is common to all. For example, in order to draw a conclusion concerning a certain disease we need to examine its symptoms and effects on hundreds or even thousands of people sick with the same malady. If investigation of all the sick reveals the same beginning and the same ending, we may then come to a common judgment about it. Let us therefore investigate the origin of the up-and-down kind of life in the experience of the average

Christian and learn from it some definitive rule.

We know that the life of a believer commences with his being saved. When a person is born again, is he very sad? On the contrary, he is most happy, because on the first day that a man finds any treasure he usually is exultant. The same is true with respect to the newly saved. The day when a person is told that by believing in Jesus Christ he has received eternal life—having passed out of death into life and is thus condemned no more—is the happiest day of his life. May I ask, however, if this happiness lasts forever? No, it lasts only for a while. Such happy feeling will eventually pass away. How long, though, will it last? It varies according to different people. From what I am able to observe, such an exuberant, happy sensation rarely continues beyond a few months. Usually it remains for a month or two; and for some individuals it may last for only a week or two. Sooner or later the joyous feeling of one's salvation will fade away.

Suppose we draw a horizontal line to represent the life experience of us Christians. What is above the line can be labeled joy, what is below the line can be marked dryness. And let us say that here is a man who has had several months' joy after initially being saved. But on a certain morning while reading the Bible, praying, and communing with God as is his usual practice, he notices that his joy is not as yesterday's was. Somehow it has decreased. Now it is quite true that after being saved some believers are subject to persecution and ill-treatment, others have to deal with sins and make restitution and offer apologies—and yet they possess joy unspeakable which more than compensates for all these losses. Without any doubt everyone ought to be joyous at being saved; even God rejoices over each person's salvation. But was it not true in your own experience that a few months after your conversion, your joy gradually faded away? You no longer felt as happy as before. When first saved, your delight was in reading the Bible. Though you may not have understood its full meaning, you nonetheless enjoyed reading its pages. It was not too much for you in those days to have read tens of chapters a day. The same applied to prayer. You were most happy with prayer. Whether your prayers were answered or not, you still loved to pray. You could shut yourself in a room for several hours and commune with God. Sometimes you might even have leapt for joy. But all that is now in the past; for today you do not feel joyous anymore. You are sad.

At this juncture in your spiritual experience two temptations may come to you: one may come from the enemy, in that Satan may accuse you by saying you have fallen, even that you have not been saved; the other may come from yourself, because you may conclude that since you have fallen you must have committed some sin—and yet in searching wherein you may have sinned you cannot find anything in particular. Nonetheless, the dry and barren state continues.

Yet such dryness oftentimes will not last long. Sometimes it is over in one or two weeks, and sometimes it may last for but three or four days. And as soon as the dry spell passes, your joy returns to you. During the season of dryness your Bible reading and your praying seemed to have been dragged out by force as though you had been trying merely to recite something which you could not remember. But now you feel your communion with God is renewed and refreshed. Yet how this restoration came about is a mystery to you. And hence you presently resolve to be more careful in retaining your joy. You must now exert all your strength to preserve this exultant feeling. You will be more diligent in reading God's word, in prayer, and in witnessing.

Surprisingly, though, not long afterwards your joy again disappears. You recall how you read the Bible and prayed and witnessed today as much as you did yesterday—yea, even more; why then is there such a vast difference between the two days? Why, you ask yourself, did you have joy yesterday but do not have it today? In such a situation you now are not sure of yourself—not even sure are you of God and of Jesus Christ. And then you make one of the biggest mistakes of your life: you think you have lost your spiritual power and have fallen. Though you still pray, you do so unfaithfully; though you read the Bible, it is only briefly; and though you witness, it is forced. What is a marvel to you is that after a few days or a few weeks, the earlier joy once more returns to you. Once again you take pleasure in doing everything. Though it may not be an experience of the third heaven, you nevertheless have the experience of being on a mountain top. Yet what becomes even more puzzling to you is that after a while you fall into a dry and tasteless condition for still *another* time. For this reason you cannot help but conjecture that life is truly full of ebbs and tides. If anyone should currently inquire about your spiritual state you would most likely answer that your life is definitely full of highs and lows: What you deem to be a high is when you read the Bible, pray, and witness with joy and pleasure: What you reckon to be a low is when you feel tasteless and dry in doing the same things. This is what you call a high-and-low life.

Let us review from the very beginning, then, how it is that a believer gets into these high and low situations. If we can ferret out the cause, we will obtain the healing. And in searching through the experiences of many born-again people I believe we discover one basic law—which is, that joy decreases from much to little while dryness increases from less to more. The intensity of joy gradually dissipates (though it becomes increasingly deeper) and in addition the season of that joy grows shorter and shorter; whereas the intensity of dryness increases with time and its season gets longer and longer (though it becomes increasingly shallow). Perhaps the first dryness lasts for only three or four days; the second dryness, for a week; the third dryness, for two weeks; and the fourth dryness, for as long as an entire month. In other words, the second joy is shorter and less intense than the first, but the second dryness lasts longer and is more concentrated than the first one. Seasons of dryness become longer, and intensity of dryness increases with time. All believers have this kind of experience. In short, Christians encounter more dryness than joy.

Is there any Christian nowadays who can say that his joy today exceeds that of the first day on which he was saved? How we believers are troubled in our hearts! We feel we have sinned and are defeated. We do not have as much joy as at the time of our initial salvation. When we were first saved we felt as though we were riding on the clouds and skipping atop the mountains. How bold we were in witnessing, even witnessing on the street. We could read 50 or 60 chapters of the Bible a day and still consider that insufficient. But currently our feeling is quite different. Everything is done unenthusiastically and by compulsion.

Let me observe that we commit a basic blunder here. How seriously we misunderstand spiritual experience: for with hardly any exception we all infer that joyous feeling represents spiritual height: but as a matter of fact, dryness of heart does not *necessarily* mean spiritual ebb. Allow me to illustrate this point as follows: When I find my lost watch, I feel most happy. A few days later, however, my joy will not be as buoyant as when I first found my watch. And perhaps within a few more days, this joy has completely faded away. Yet at that moment my watch has not been lost again. What has happened here? Simply this, that what is now lost is not my watch once again but the joy at finding the watch in the first place! Let me say that it is the same with our spiritual experience. When a person finds the Savior and is saved, he cannot but be joyous. (If anyone lacks joy at the time of salvation, I must wonder if he has actually found the Savior.) Later, though, when he loses his joyful feeling, he may think he has also lost the thing he had earlier rejoiced in. Here is what we all need to recognize; namely, that although the believer's joyful feeling has been lost, the object of that joy has not been lost.

Let me ask you this, Has the Lord Jesus changed? Not at all. Has God changed? No, He has not. Has God retrieved the eternal life that He once gave to you? Of course not, for both when you feel excited and when you even feel dry, you still have the same eternal life. However excited or uninspired you may feel, your situation remains the same, because the thing which you received from God is never lost. Therefore, I may say that there is really no such thing as a high-and-low situation in a Christian's life and experience. (This cannot apply, of course, to those Christians who have really sinned and fallen away. They are the exception. What is mentioned here is applicable only to Christians in a general way.)

God never changes, neither does the work of the Lord Jesus know any change, nor does the Holy Spirit ever change. The eternal life you received is still there. What subsequently changes or is lost is the joyful feeling you experienced at the time of salvation. For example, a child in his ignorance thinks that the sun has disappeared on a rainy day. So he asks his father where the sun went. He climbs the stairs to gain a higher view of the sun, but he cannot find it. He may even ascend a watchtower nearby, yet still he cannot find the sun. In actuality, though, we older ones know that the sun has not changed: it has merely been hidden from view by dark clouds. Now in just the same way, the believer's Sun has not changed, only his feeling has: there are dark clouds in his personal sky so that the light of his Sun is screened from view. If a believer lives in his feeling, his sky will often change and be frequently over-shadowed by clouds. But if he does not live according to feeling, his sky will suffer no change at all. We ought to live above the dark clouds of feeling.

We have already said that the intensity of joy decreases and its season shortens as time goes on, while the intensity of dryness increases with time and its season lengthens. This is a common phenomenon shared by all Christians. There is nothing accidental about it. Many saints have the same experience. Since this is not something accidental, there must be a hand behind it which arranges it. Whose hand is it? It is the hand of God. It is God who causes the intensity of our joy to decrease and shorten with time. And it is He who makes the intensity of our dryness to increase and lengthen with time.

As to abnormal Christians, that is to say, as to those who have sinned and fallen away, they naturally have no joy. To those superior Christians who seek God with singleness from the very start and who lay themselves down without reservation, they experience special joy after each new endeavor. Every time they see the work of God, they enter into special joy. Both the abnormal and superior are the exception. I speak here only to Christians in general.

God's Aims

What are God's aims in arranging such conditions in our Christian experience? These aims are as follows:

(1) *To show you that you are to do nothing for your own sake.* When you are excited and joyful, you read the Bible with relish. Are you reading it because it is the word of God or do you read it because it is tasteful to you? What is the aim of your prayer? Is it to go before God and seek Him for His own sake or is it to derive pleasure from your prayer? Do you pray for God's sake or do you desert your duty to pray? If what you do is all for the latter reasons, then you do all these in order to satisfy yourself. Your aim is not for the glory of God.

In your zeal you may not feel you are undertaking a thing for your own sake but think you are doing so for God. Nevertheless, you should remember that at the time of great excitement as though you were on cloud nine, you may perhaps be most fleshly! Hence God takes away your joy and puts you in a dry state. How *then* do you feel? Your prayer, Bible reading, and witnessing now seem to be rather forced. God places you in such a situation in order to teach you a lesson; that you may come to realize that what you feel about a mountain-top experience as being that which is most spiritual is after all self-motivated. What you consider to be the most spiritual of experiences turns out to be actually something fleshly. Formerly you exhibited the bad side of your flesh to the world: currently you are exhibiting the good side of the same flesh. God desires to show you whether you will still pray or read the Bible or witness when there is no joy but only dryness. Even so, He does not want you to be overly oppressed by aridity, and hence He once again gives you joy. And once more you regard your spiritual life as touching the peak, with the result that He takes your joy away a second time. But after a short while God returns to you a little joy lest you become discouraged by your parched and tasteless state and are ready to give up as a Christian.

When the second dry spell comes upon you, God may ask you if you have found out anything. You think this is again due to your own fault. But in fact that is not God's aim in all this. What He aims at is to help you to determine whether you are doing these things out of Christian duty or out of joy. For some people it may probably take five or six times, even seven or eight times, or may require repeated cycles of joy and aridity before God is able to attain His aim in them. He wants them to know that they usually look for joy for their own sake, not for the sake of God. This is the first reason why the Lord gives us this treatment of joy-and-dryness.

(2) *To train our will power.** When you are having mountain-top experiences, do you find it hard to

---

*The will power mentioned here is the power of the will that wills the will of God. It is strengthened by the Holy Spirit through exercise.—*Translator*

do things? You most certainly do not. It does not take any effort of yours to read the Bible, to pray, or to witness. For example, suppose you are naturally talkative. When you are most rapturous—sensing the closeness of God as though you could touch the Lord Jesus himself—you reflect that it is best if you shut yourself in a room and see no one from dawn to dusk. During such a time, it is almost instinctive for you to overcome your natural weakness of being talkative. Or suppose, as another example, that you are a quick-tempered person and are usually easily provoked into anger. At the time of elation, you can forgive people without much difficulty. Yet as soon as your joy fades away, you react like a porcupine. You explode whenever people touch you. Or still another example, during a period of excitement you experience no hardship in living and working; but just you find yourself in a dry spell and you will discover that you face tremendous pressure in both areas so that it takes strong will power for you to read the Bible, to pray, and to witness: indeed, you have to remind yourself constantly that it is your duty to perform such acts. Formerly, inspired by the intensity of your rapturous feeling, you could speak for five hours non-stop. But now you feel so listless that you have not one word to say. You seem to be bound when you try to tell people how to believe in the Lord Jesus and be saved. You have to force yourself into speaking. Unless you really *want* to do things, you are unable to do them.

Right here I must raise this important question. When is the time that we really pass through spiritual experience? In the moment of great joy on high or during the period of dryness in the valley below? Is it not when we are in a dry season? For at the time of excitement, we are carried along in the current of our emotion: it cannot be viewed as a spiritual experience. But when we feel dry, we must exercise our *will*; and therefore whatever we do in such a situation it is the real person, the real I, who does it. The reason why God gives you and me a dry spell is to cause us to exercise the power of our will.

If, for instance, we board a sailboat to go to a certain place, usually we will arrive in a few hours. When we first start out, the wind is probably blowing quite forcefully. So we happily set sail for our destination. In a short while, however, the wind may stop without our reaching the place intended—there are still a few hours of sailing distance left. What, now, are we to do? Should we row the boat with oars? Or should we cast anchor and wait for the wind again? Well, if we expect an early arrival we must row with all our strength. And during such a time we will be using our real strength. Now this is but an illustration of this second aim of God—to train us to exercise our will power. When our emotions are stirred up, it is like a boat sailing before the wind—its sailors needing to exercise no labor at all. How we believers anticipate the help of such a wind all through our lives. But in a sailboat such action would reduce the captain and his sailors to uselessness. If they were to decide either to sail only with the wind or else to do nothing, who would ever engage such sailors? We thank God when he gives us the forceful winds of our emotion to carry us through at times. But God also desires to stimulate us into exercising the resurrection power He has given us. Otherwise we shall not move if we have no joyful feeling. Consequently, God gives dryness so that we may use the strength which we receive at regeneration and move on even without the help of joyful and rapturous feeling. And thus will we be able to sail through our Christian life even if there be no wind. For the power of resurrection is made more manifest in the midst of deprivation and death.

Emotional help may be granted to us, nevertheless that is not God's aim. It is merely part of the process by which God deals with us. What He aims at is to train our will so that at the darkest hour we are able to exercise our will power. When we feel dry, we may nevertheless use our will to read the Bible, to pray, and to witness. Through repeated exercises the power of the will will become stronger and stronger. If we only proceed with emotional power throughout our life we will never make much progress. The reason God gives us joyous feelings is to prevent us from becoming so discouraged as to turn back from being Christians. But then He will gradually decrease and shorten our joy and also increase and lengthen our dryness so that we may exercise our will power until we ourselves become strong.

As we review our past experience we shall notice that our joy and dryness come upon us like waves. We also discover that we do not make much progress in time of joy whereas we make more progress in time of dryness. We see ourselves actually advance during that dry week. How we used to think we had fallen if daily our lives were so harsh and tasteless! But when we honestly compare our experiences we will find that we make progress when we feel weak but make little progress when we are joyous. When the wind blows hard and we sail with the wind, will it help us to use our arm strength? Certainly not, for it is not needed. We always must use more arm strength when there is no wind or when we sail against the wind. Our progress depends much on how we exercise our will power. When we feel dry, let us use the power of our will—declaring " I *want* to advance"—and we shall advance indeed. How very sad that the eyes of many believers are fixed on this center of joy, deeming it to be the peak of spiritual experience; but they fail to understand that the Christian makes real spiritual progress when he moves on in the power of his will.

(3) *To have us overcome environment*. If you can overcome the feeling of aridity, you will be able to overcome your environment. For a dry and listless sensation is the hardest to surmount. By overcoming it, you can quite naturally overcome other environments. The most intimate of all environments is your emotion. If you are able to conquer your emotion, you will be victorious over other environments too. You ought to exercise the power of the will by saying, I *will* read the Bible, I *will* pray, and I *will* witness. Though you may live in dryness without any sense of anointing, you nonetheless shall discover the

power to vanquish anything in your environment, however big that thing may be. May I speak frankly and say that whoever cannot overcome environment has not overcome emotion. He who conquers environment has first conquered his own feelings.

(4) *To have us live by faith.* The seasons of joy grow shorter and those of dryness become longer. The intensity of joy gradually decreases while that of dryness increases—until there comes a day when the two meet as at the confluence of two water currents, so that all distinctions disappear. They finally flow together and become one, each indistinguishable from the other. God's aim in leading us this way is to show us that these two actually are no different at all. In other words, our joy and dryness merge and become one. Today God has this purpose that the just shall live by faith and not live by feeling. However we may feel, that does not give us anything. With some believers, God has to train them 10 or even 20 times to cause them not to live by their emotional strength. He allows their dryness to grow longer and intensify deeper so as to lead them to the place where they can live by faith. If you have never been trained, you will soon discover how utterly powerless your emotional strength is. For the just shall only live by faith.

Finally, if you do learn to live by faith, you may live the most joyous life in the midst of aridity—and the most tasteless life in the midst of felicity. This may sound paradoxical, yet this is a truth in spiritual life. God will lead us to live the life of faith.

What is meant by living by faith? It is represented to us very clearly by the words spoken to Nebuchadnezzar by the Hebrews Shadrach, Meshach and Abednego: "Our God whom we serve is able to deliver us from the burning fiery furnace; and he will deliver us out of thy hand, O king. But if not, be it known unto thee, O king, that we will not serve thy gods, nor worship the golden image which thou hast set up" (Dan. 3.17–18). What they meant was that even if God should not save them, they would not be affected, they would not change. *That* is what is meant to live by faith!

Christians nowadays incline too strongly towards a life of feeling. If God should take away their joyous feeling, they would lose everything. Yet God does not say to live by feeling but He says to live by faith. After years of experience you will come to realize that joy and dryness are really the same. No great outburst of joy will affect you, nor will any moment of dryness influence you. You live the same life through deep aridity as well as through great joy.

Oh that we may not act like those with a small capacity—in joy they dance in the house; in dryness they drench the wall with tears. If we live by faith we shall not be swayed by either of them. Even so, let it be plainly understood that we are not people without emotion. We do have feelings of joy as well as of dryness. But we ought not allow these external sensations to touch our inward man; for what we have been stressing in this message to young believers today is that the joy which the outward man feels is not that which the inward man enjoys in the Lord, because this latter joy is most deep and unshakable. Yet this deep and unshakable joy is not experienced fully until we are able to control completely this outward joy. May the Lord be able to achieve His aims in us so that we may live by faith and not by feeling.